MW01143202

AWAKENING YOUR
OPTIMAL WORKFORCE

AWAKENING YOUR OPTIMAL WORKFORCE

Prioritize Well-Being and Living at Our Best Consistently

Mark Hattas
and the Optimal Being team

ISBN: 978-0-9994815-4-7

To all the leaders who care for their teams,

*To all team members who care to live, work, and play
in this sandbox of life at their very best,*

To YOU!

Contents

Introduction

Leaders of an awakened workforce know their organization can thrive only when its people thrive.

An awakened workforce is available to everyone. It contains common elements across every company, factory, or breakroom. Organizations with an awakened workforce know these elements and foster a supportive workplace for their fulfillment. Awakened leaders understand the elements are foundational for thriving in today's world, both professionally and personally.

This type of organization will be commonplace, yet today, few companies support the principles necessary for an awakened workforce to show up.

Imagine what may exist within the walls of an organization. Though an unsubstantiated legend, Michelangelo was apparently asked about the difficulties he encountered in sculpting his masterpiece *David*.

He supposedly replied, "It is easy. You just chip away the stone that doesn't look like David."

Likewise, your awakened workforce exists in the people working for your company now. The question is how to bring it to the surface and sustain it.

This book answers that question. There is a process available to support your people consistently living in their awakened state. Another benefit: Your organization will thrive as a result of doing so. Furthermore, your workforce will be engaged, be happy, and be able to thrive, no matter the circumstances. When new situations along the way appear potentially troublesome, the workforce who has tools to master the elements of well-being will bounce back faster, stay in an optimal flow state longer, live a more joyous existence, and together, create something truly spectacular.

Now that employee well-being has become a top priority in most companies, it is time to learn how to identify what true well-being is. Once you've gained that understanding, the actions needed to support well-being in the workplace will be obvious to you. In this book, you learn the ten key elements of well-being and how to discern the difference between someone behaving on autopilot or being conscious and present. Additionally, the book leads you to tools and resources that support living consistently in your optimal state.

In the following chapters, we illustrate well-being elements of an awakened workforce through a fictional story. "Ethan" represents the Guides and Mentors of our team as he interviews members of Easy Breezy, our fictional company. The employees he interviews share stories inspired by experiences of persons who have journeyed through our Optimal Being curriculum. Each character represents a different element, and their stories draw on the highly statistically significant results for actual participants.

The ten elements of well-being have been described in numerous ways across many disciplines, so you may be familiar with some or all of the elements. We invite you to expand your understanding and integrate these elements into your life experience. Each element is represented as a strength or a challenge in you and every person. The combination of all ten elements, including strengths and challenges, reveals a personal code that dictates how each of us shows up in any given situation, especially when under stress.

In a perfect world, all ten elements of someone's personal code would be strengths. However, like anything people attempt to master, the process does not have a finish line. The pianist who spends ten-thousand-plus hours performing and practicing will be a more delightful performer than a person in their first thousand hours of training. Yet, both musicians have an opportunity to learn, grow, and evolve even further. Likewise, each participant in our program will always have opportunities to learn, practice, and evolve their personal code.

Unfortunately, most of us have acquired some poor habits in life. These habits are revealed through this personal code. They appear as the top challenges impacting our overall well-being. These challenges continue playing out in a person's life as patterns of negative and destructive behaviors again and again . . . you get the idea. People who successfully address the challenges in their personal code realize an end to misery and pain. They experience courage, strength, joy, and clarity. They live as optimal beings.

If you were unaware that employees are having challenges at work, in society, and in life on so many fronts, you probably wouldn't be reading this book. So, good on you for showing up! Good on you for being present enough to know an issue exists!

Let's play a game. This game requires a piece of paper and a pen. Yes, get a piece of paper and something to write with or work with the table right in the book. Ready?

Draw a line down the middle of the paper to create two halves. In the top left, write the words *Optimal State (in alignment)*. Below this, on the left half, write words that reflect a human being living in their optimal state. Do this now and return to reading once you have completed this step.

Next, on the top right-hand side of the page write *Out of Alignment*, and below this, write words that remind you of someone when they are not in their ideal state. Do this and come back when complete.

Optimal State (in alignment)	Out of Alignment

This exercise has been done thousands of times and was shared with us by Dr. Michael Ryce (whyagain.org). While everyone's answers are slightly different, a common theme emerges. The *Optimal State* side typically has words that reflect some version of love. You may have included happy, joyful, integrity, respect, trust, love, beautiful, engaged, or other words. These words reflect our Optimal Being state of living. In contrast, the *Out of Alignment* side always has some variation of anger, hate, hurt, fear, envy, jealousy, betrayal, grief, or sadness. Oh my! *What an uggghly list*!

Of course, like all human beings, you have experienced yourself and others in an optimal state, and you have experienced yourself and others out of alignment. I don't need to ask which you like better. Life is more fulfilling and fun when we, and the people around us, are living as Optimal Beings.

People can flash in and out of alignment during a single conversation. Others live out of alignment, or in their nonbeing state, so often that people think that is who they are. Life is bumpy in that non-being state. People in this state are stressed, overwhelmed, unhappy, and feel out of control in life, hopelessly waiting for something to change or some job or someone to save them from misery. Such a state paints a bleak picture, but a potentially mutable one.

In fact, some who find themselves out of alignment are able to shift into an optimal state effortlessly. These people experience living as an Optimal Being more often and have tools and resources to support restoration when something interrupts it. They may have a down day, but rarely a down week. Living in this manner may or may not sound like you now, but anyone can achieve this experience. The stories you read here will show numerous examples of challenges in each area of well-being. With a bit of practice, mastering well-being becomes enjoyable, and eventually, quite effortless.

Imagine if we could bring the lessons of living as an Optimal Being to everyone in every organization. What if our entire workforce had the resources to live as their Optimal Being consistently? Utopia? No, not the way utopia is often thought of, where everyone and everything is always perfect. No, that is not what is going to happen.

What *will* happen is described in these pages. People will have everything they need to live in their optimal state more frequently than they did before, until it is natural for them to be in that state. And, if people ever move out of alignment, and it will happen, the only priority will be restoration to alignment, to an Optimal Being state of living.

Of course, you can't make anyone be in this state. You can't mandate that everyone must use the tools in this book. You are not able to—nor would you want to—force anything on anyone. As a leader, you *can* be an example of what it's like to live in an optimal state. You *can* offer an opportunity for every person in your workforce to benefit in a way that will serve them at work, home, and everywhere in life. You *can* even offer it to others beyond the walls of your organization. You *can* be a vessel through which families of your workforce find resources and tools supporting them as they live their very best lives.

If someone at your company has invited you to read this book and you have read this far, you are likely the perfect person to be reading it. As people who practice Optimal Being and desire to be with others who also practice, we share common ground. Here you are. Here I am. And here are all who practice Optimal Being.

This adventure supports you in appreciating how wonderful your life actually can be. Give it a chance. Live a little. Love a little. Laugh a little. And then, do it some more. You were made in the image of love and so were all your cohorts at work and home.

I hope one day I can see you and everyone as Optimal Beings and do so in each moment. The journey has many rewards, no matter your destination. The life you have always known is in you is available, and this is where it begins. Let us introduce you to the ten elements of living your best life, now.

Let's begin by meeting Ethan and the Easy Breezy company.

Chapter 1

Ethan: The Interviews

If a hose in your garden is kinked and the flow is low, you would certainly find the kink and address it. Would you do the same with your well-being if it had a kink? I am committing to this, and I invite you to join me on this journey.

~ Yori, CEO, Easy Breezy

The Easy Breezy company faced choices it never anticipated, and those choices appeared when their financials had taken a significant hit. Employees felt largely out of sorts and stressed, and they faced uncertainty like never before. These challenges weren't just at work. The world was chaotic at best, and some were facing crises at home. During 2020, issues related to well-being had reached exhausting numbers. Those issues impacted people's work settings, requiring many to stay at home and work remotely. Some loved working at home, while others hated it.

Easy Breezy wanted people back at the office, yet also considered options to allow leases to lapse. People realized life would never be the same but wondered what changes would last long term. Bigger issues than office space loomed large. Topics once hidden were at the surface. Conflicts once muted were loud. Areas of pain were being exposed and growth opportunities were apparent. This was new for everyone, including leadership, who searched for solutions. They started by looking within.

A confidential survey revealed 80 percent of their employees were experiencing symptoms of anxiety and depression. The hope that normal was going to return on its own was dimming. This startling insight coincided with a report that Easy Breezy's number-one increase in cost in 2019, well before the pandemic, was medication. The 2020 numbers were worse, as employees who had never had issues were feeling overwhelmed, anxious, disoriented, angry, sad, and scared. Others seemed to be getting by, but were they actually all right?

Just when leaders at Easy Breezy thought no more surprises could come, another would peek its head around the corner. Some people hid or numbed their pain. Others grinned and bore it. A few were vocal, sinking in life and asking for help. Even fewer seemed to be navigating rather well through the storm. Overall, they couldn't take much more. Something needed to change. For the first time ever, employee well-being became the organization's number-one priority.

Easy Breezy's Chief HR Officer (CHRO), Randy Bruce, saw this coming, and he wasn't alone. A consulting friend of his shared poll results of 650 CHROs from major corporations, most with billion-dollar-plus valuations. They collectively agreed workforce well-being was their number-one priority.

Being a data guy, Randy dove deep beyond their internal surveys in preparation of a board presentation on actionable options. Some of the uglier data: 52 percent of Americans have tried to grin and bear it instead of seeking help when feeling depressed or mentally unstable.[1] Worse, those who do seek help tend to first struggle with symptoms eight to ten years on average.[2] This might explain the high number of disengaged employee statistics (70 percent by some accounts).[3]

It's one thing for an employee to show up *for* work, but quite another for one to fully show up and engage while *at* work. People's issues remain largely hidden until the pain of keeping quiet outweighs the pain of saying or doing something about it. Unfortunately, by that time a metaphoric Mount Vesuvius is about to blow. Though millennials seem more comfortable discussing these topics, only one in three employees ever gets the help they need.[4]

Like many organizations, Easy Breezy felt they had made a sincere effort to support mental and emotional well-being and yet, only 6.9 percent of their employees were using the EAP (employee assistance program) as they were either concerned with confidentiality, had trouble navigating the options, or didn't understand what it was.[5] Something else was needed. EAP wasn't enough. The fitness center and other wellness solutions were not enough.

As Yori, Easy Breezy's CEO, listened intently to Randy's presentation of the data, he recalled the face of a computer programmer he knew, Ozzie. Within hours of the board meeting's conclusion, Ozzie and Yori discussed Ozzie's obvious transformation since completing the Optimal Being program. Ozzie had continued practicing the tools, and Yori could see the program was clearly working for him. The two of them went to Randy and outlined the possible benefits of applying Optimal Being throughout Easy Breezy. They soon reached an agreement to bring in the program through Journey's Dream.

Journey's Dream is a nonprofit resource hub for sustained mental health serving individuals and corporations. Easy Breezy loved how Journey's Dream views every person on a continuum of health. At one end, people are thriving and living in their optimal state. These people are swimming confidently and aren't looking for help or support on a daily basis, but they could still benefit from well-being tools for the days when life throws them a curve.

In the middle of the continuum, the next group is struggling somewhere between treading water and floating. They need support, whether they are seeking it or not. At the opposite end of the spectrum, the last group has stopped floating and is sinking or sank a while back. Though this last group may have people diagnosed with mental health disorders, that is often not the case. Either way, Journey's Dream presented a mental and emotional hygiene model supporting everyone living in their optimal state more consistently. Their solutions led to people thriving in life with tools for sustained well-being.

The anticipation of the program's start just seven months ago was mixed. Some loved it. Some didn't understand why it was needed. Others rejected it. Despite the mixed reception, the program was launched with a portion of the executive team first. They chose to lead by example. A second group was a quick start of participants who were open to being Internal Trainers as the program rolled out across the organization.

After this successful start, it was obvious that continuing was the right thing for Easy Breezy. The next group, and then the next, kicked off. Easy Breezy allowed for people to sign up as early adopters and otherwise introduced it to teams having the greatest challenges first. The results? You will hear for yourself in the following interviews.

In fact, let's listen in as Ethan, our interviewer, kicks things off.

*

Welcome to the Easy Breezy company, where ten employees volunteered to be interviewed, each representing one of ten elements of well-being necessary for an awakened workforce.

These interviews highlight the experiences of individuals who struggled with an element—their top challenge—as they practiced the principles taught in the Optimal Being program. This program is a hybrid learning model that supports people in living their optimal lives. As you read through the transcripts of these interviews, you will find the question is not whether someone can live as their Optimal Being and experience life at its fullest, but how willing someone is to do so, consistently supporting themself, others, and their organization in the process.

My name is Ethan, and I happened upon these extraordinary tools when I needed them most.

I will be conducting the interview series and am so thankful for the opportunity to do so. Not long ago, I was in real trouble. My life was at a crossroads. I was having suicidal thoughts and wanted desperately to stop the pain.

One day, a total stranger asked if I was considering hurting myself. I answered, "Yes, but how did you know?"

She said that was not important, but what was important was *me*. She shared her story and offered to help me hear what I wanted most in life. Within an hour, I received the first of many insights. She called me occasionally until I asked if I could learn what she was teaching me. I don't know why I didn't ask sooner, but *better late than never*, right? She told me about the Optimal Being program, the same program our volunteers completed over the past several months.

As I learned the principles and practiced the tools you will hear about soon, more insights arrived, though I didn't always see them right away. They were often subtle. One day, that stranger and now friend, Angie, asked if I wanted to hurt myself anymore. I hadn't even realized it before she asked, but the suicidal thoughts had gone. Also, there was this pure version of me that showed up more frequently—a happy version.

After volunteering at Journey's Dream to give back to the organization that helped me, my mastery of the tools grew, and I offered to help deliver these tools to people in their workplaces. With my background in film, they asked me to spend some time at Easy Breezy and interview program graduates. I can attest they have been doing the work. The results are evident.

You will find a theme in their stories. See if you can find it in all of them. When a well-being element moves into alignment, new awareness always follows. Participants might have seen the world one way, and now they see it another. The way they perceive others changes. Their lifelong behaviors shift, and it is always for their benefit.

Before interviewing the ten Easy Breezy employees, my film team and I set up in a corner conference room at the end of a hallway of offices. We brought in chairs, side tables, lights, and a couple of cameras. This ninth-floor view, overlooking the city's arboretum, offered a spectacular treetop backdrop of reds, yellows, and oranges, celebrating the change of seasons from summer to fall.

Each person interviewed represents someone who began the program challenged by a particular element. They will share their experience as they moved through those challenges and completed the Optimal Being program, applying its practices and tools. Keep in mind, these interviews are not with people who are masters in these areas, but instead have made marked improvements in their lives.

Each person has their own dynamic personality and their own reason for sharing. I found they all care deeply about growth and experiencing a life filled with more happiness and fulfillment. Most of these interviewees have kept their same responsibilities at work following the program, but they now experience the opportunity much differently. Transformations in the areas they share ignited new perceptions for them with fresh insights about the organization as well.

For anonymity, these employees have chosen names reflective of the element they focused on.

As you witness their transformations, I hope you are as inspired by their journeys as I am. Remember, this path is available to you and your organization's workforce as well.

Let's get started!

Chapter 2

Harmony: Stress Management

Harmony picked a name representing balance and peace in contrast to the stress and occasional overwhelm she had become used to.

Harmony works in order fulfillment, ensuring orders are correctly filled in a timely manner. Hers is a quick-paced job, requiring constant focus on details and attentiveness to accuracy and speed.

As Harmony entered the room, I was struck by her relaxed, easy walk. The folds of her long, sea-green skirt softly swayed in silence, and I was reminded of ocean waves. She shook her hair loose from a clip, and her face erupted in a smile. As her name highlights, she exhibited true balance, peace, and harmony.

The Interview

Good morning, Harmony. Thank you for being here today to discuss the well-being element of stress management! Welcome.

Oh, thank you so much.

I'd like to begin by asking you to describe this first element, stress management.

That's funny to me now, because managing stress is actually quite impossible.

What do you mean impossible?

Well . . . Have you ever tried to manage what you smell? Imagine smelling garbage, and then trying to *manage* what you are smelling. Impossible.

I see what you mean. It's just there, and if you are breathing, you are smelling it.

Right, so the way to change what you are smelling is to notice the source of the smell, and in this case, take out the trash. If you are not able to take it out, you can accept the smell or move from the source. Stress is similar: Notice it, find the source of it, and take action. What you *can* manage are the source goals, expectations, beliefs, and assumptions, but managing stress is not likely. When the gap widens between the way we want something to be and the way it actually is, our stress increases. Like smelling the trash, our body clues us in when there is a gap between the way we want it, fresh smell, and the way it actually is, stinky. We all *feel* stress in our bodies through sensations: butterflies, sweats, headaches, tension . . .

For me, stress definitely rises in my gut with everything from butterflies to nausea. In the past, I would try to ignore the feelings or find a way to prevent them. Sometimes I drank. Sometimes I lashed out in anger. It worked for a short time. But I was damaging relationships, and it wasn't worth it just to feel better for a short while. In the program, we called anger *the most accessible drug on the planet*. It is a s*hort-term anesthesia*, numbing the experience. I still get angry, but thankfully, I feel more equipped to address it at the root cause before it erupts. It's way more enjoyable for me and others.

Well said, Harmony! Would you be willing to share more about your past—what you were like before? It sounds like things got pretty rough.

Yes and yes. In the past, tension would mount, but I was not aware of what was happening until it was too late. My reactions then kicked in automatically. I now see I was afraid of it, of myself; that acknowledging it sooner might make it worse. So, I'd try to stay calm and cover up the growing anxiety. I actually thought I was good at it, but, in the end, I wound up panicking, often blurting something out that was, shall we say, unconstructive. Then, I'd feel ashamed and guilty. When I got home, I would numb myself. Even though my family life was struggling, the first thing I'd want to do at home was open a bottle of wine or have a cocktail.

At first, my husband mixed amazing cocktails for me; he just wanted me to feel happier. He didn't like me being anxious and stressed either. With that first sip, my system let down as if saying: *Okay, we can relax now.* In the end, my drinking became such an issue that my husband was on the verge of asking for a divorce.

Harmony paused as her eyes welled up. She took a nice, deep breath. I waited patiently for her to continue. She took a few more breaths, and I saw her body relax back in the chair. Guides in the program learn to give people space to process thoughts, emotions, and memories and offer support when invited. My role is often to breathe with them as they use the tools learned in the program. I could tell she was using them as we sat in silence. Harmony nodded a signal that she was ready and continued talking about her husband.

Bless the man. He took responsibility for everything in our home for years. I couldn't have told you what our kids were doing in school at that time. Even the strongest of people have breaking points, though, and I pushed him to the limit, to an edge that has no return for many. I was frustrated with myself because I knew I could do better. I wouldn't say that I was an alcoholic, but others did. I now see I didn't have the tools I needed to address the unhealthy stresses in my life. I feel so much happier now.

Wow. That is a heavy story and topic, and incredibly encouraging. Thank you, Harmony.

My eyes teared up a little in celebration, as she was clearly on a healthier path. Over the years, I've heard this type of story repeatedly. The ability to shift from unhealthy and dysfunctional stress to optimal and healthy stress will transform anyone.

Can you pinpoint a moment when you realized you could be conscious of the stress symptoms early enough to accept their interruption and do something about it?

Oh, for sure. That took place in my yard, June of last year. An unhappy neighbor was walking up the driveway. Apparently, there were some Homeowners Association (HOA) covenants we had broken when we put up a shed in our backyard. As the neighbor spoke, I sensed this energy building in me; I was noticing she had been holding back and was about to let me have it. I was impressed that I noticed it immediately. I smiled, though that wasn't necessarily the best approach in that moment. It encouraged the woman to increase the volume of her voice and her attack because she thought I was making light of her concern. What I was actually doing was enjoying the awareness of the disruption.

When I recognized the feelings—stomach tightness and holding my breath—I released my hold and continued to breathe consciously, allowing all my feelings to be felt. She continued to attack, and as she spoke, I asked myself what I wanted. The first answer: I wanted her to go away. I did not like being attacked. I let that go and realized what I really wanted was for this woman to accept our shed as it was.

You see, I hadn't gone to the HOA. Neither my husband nor I even thought about it. So, there I was, in my garage, realizing I wanted this woman to just accept it was okay. My tension really increased, and I was doing my best to breathe. In the past, I would have said she "made me tense," but I know better now. If I'm feeling something, it's *in* me. Essentially, she couldn't *cause* my pain. I knew something in me was *off*. I needed to release my goal for her to accept my shed as it was. As long as I hung on to that goal, I would stay in a battle, looking for ways to defend myself to get what I wanted. Once I let go of needing the situation to be different, I was able to accept that she was upset and actually listen. She wanted people to follow the rules. She wanted justice.

Within a couple of moments, I felt calm. It was a bit surreal. She was still yelling, but it was like I was witnessing it from a distance, and the typical reaction didn't come. I felt compassion for her and our neighbors. I remembered how I would get so upset like her with other people. Through the program, I discovered how I did that when I was in pain.

I will always remember the next moment. I allowed her to continue for a bit and then held up my hand. "Uncle," I said. "You are upset, and I get it. I failed to contact the Homeowners Association. I made a mistake and broke a covenant that keeps our neighborhood looking nice. Your coming over here to let me know must not have been easy, and I appreciate you doing that before we heard from the association. Thank you. I've always liked you."

I was being honest with her. She is a lovely person, under normal circumstances.

How did she respond to that?

Her mouth opened to speak, as she was on a roll, but she caught herself and looked confused. I think she was expecting me to come right back at her. When she realized what I had said, her shoulders dropped as she stood looking at me.

During that moment of silence, a memory of my mother appeared in my mind. My mother used to berate me—just like this woman had been doing—and I would fight back. As I stood there, feeling peaceful, I saw how my neighbor represented my mother. However, I chose a new response; I didn't try to defend anything. I realized this approach could have helped my relationship with my mom.

Anyway, back to the neighbor. I interrupted the silence by asking if she would be willing to take a look at the shed and help me understand the issues. She went from hard and rigid to soft and nurturing, saying, "Oh, oh, sure. Yeah. Yeah, I'll come."

Then she walked back with me and pointed out that we had placed our shed right on the easement between properties instead of leaving the four-foot distance required. I was able to take pictures of the issue and send a letter to the association admitting our mistake. I offered to move the shed or do whatever they'd like. They were so appreciative that I brought it up because they'd received a couple of complaints and weren't sure how to approach us because we had always been such thoughtful neighbors.

They surveyed the homeowners in our vicinity, showing them the pictures and our letter, and then asked them if they were okay with us keeping it at its current location or if they wanted us to move it. We were informed in advance that if even one of the homeowners wanted a change, we would need to pour a new concrete slab and move the shed, but none did.

So, that was the moment when I realized I could stay conscious and present even under stress. It was also the moment I made a commitment to myself to make these tools a higher priority. Before that, I was kind of going through the motions, living on autopilot.

Harmony, that was incredible! Thank you. Your experience, I'm sure, will be supportive to others who want to understand the value of being in this balanced, harmonious state on a more consistent basis. I heard something worth emphasizing: Your stress has been remarkably reduced.

Oh yes! My stress was on overdrive. I still have healthy stress supporting me to get my work done, but it feels more like a friend than an enemy. I now manage goals effectively. I am way happier and more focused on what matters, and my productivity is through the roof.

I feel alive for the first time in a while, and my boss has noticed. Oh, and of course, my relationship with my husband is changing quickly for the better. I set a rule for myself that I would drink only once or twice a week, and he is helping me stick with it.

Wonderful! Is there anything else you'd like to share about the Easy Breezy organization now that you are experiencing things so differently?

Yes, I've learned to allow people to be stressed out. I noticed I was blaming people for not managing their stress as I was gaining the skill to manage mine. I just wanted to tell everyone, "Would you knock it off and just learn these tools?" That's not my place. Besides, they are just like I was a few months ago. Of course, I share when someone is interested.

That said, there's a clear difference between the people doing these practices and the ones who are not. The people doing them are much easier to be around. I'm grateful for these tools and appreciate that I work for a company making them available to everyone.

I don't know if you're aware of this, but here's an interesting stat that seventy percent of employees say work is a significant source of stress in their lives. What do you have to say about that?

Well, the only thing I would change is that most of that seventy percent *believe* work is the source of their stress. I learned the source of stress was inside of me. I used to blame work, too, which honestly allowed me to justify my most awful behaviors. Acting out had become habitual and way too comfortable, including being rather hurtful under stress. As I know well, when we make work the *cause*, we play out our victim beliefs. Work *persecutes* us in that mindset, and victims look for saviors. Who will save someone from work? Alcohol was my *savior* for a while, but it wasn't an optimal solution over time. People who blame work as their source of stress will never find peace.

People have the power to get to a peaceful state and stay there, regardless of what's happening at work. I have done the exercises for stress management hundreds of times with different sources of my stress, and every single time it turned out to be inside me. It wasn't home, or work, or my husband, or my children causing me to have stress. I denied the truth, which was one of my other challenges, but that is another topic.

Yes, we will be covering that with Alethia later today.

Oh, she and I often worked on that together. Yeah, she is such a sweetheart, and I'm sure you will have fun interviewing her. Thank you for inviting me to share today.

You are most welcome, and thank you for sharing such a wonderful example of transformation in this area of stress management. Be well.

Interview Notes

I am quite happy with my interview with Harmony. She clearly adopted the principles that support this element as a strength. She did a phenomenal job of articulating the weaknesses or what it can be like when this area is a challenge. Although she used alcohol, there are many ways people cope with their stress and unknowingly hide the actual underlying cause, consequently moving away from its source. Her story will certainly help others who face a similar challenge.

The Well-Being Element of Stress Management

If you are afflicted with stress and want solutions, they exist. Trust yourself to find what is right for you. One way you can find out if this is one of your top well-being challenges is to take the Optimal Being Personal Assessment. Not only will it identify the opportunities for you to focus on first, but it comes with insights and approaches that have proven effective for thousands of others, and certainly will for you too. Taking the assessment will certainly deepen what you learn from these interviews.

Stress is easily changed when you're aware of principles that support the change. Remember, you aren't alone. If you learn to use the Optimal Being tools, we recommend practicing with others, as Harmony and Alethia have been doing. As Harmony stated, she introduces the principles and tools to people who are interested. Sharing gives her an opportunity to strengthen what she's learned and opens up more support avenues as others also use the tools.

Would you like to more effectively navigate life when your stress is elevated? You can.

See more about stress management and how it plays out personally and organizationally when it's either a challenge or optimal by scanning this QR code using your phone's camera.

QR code URL: optimalbeing.live/well-being-info-graphic

Chapter 3

Caron: Relationship With Others

Caron chose a Welsh name that means *loving and kind-hearted*, traits much more accessible to her today.

In elementary school, there is often a place on report cards to check: *Does not play well with others*. Caron fit this characteristic, yet she has gone from destructive relationships with her workmates to relationships that are now quite healthy. Prior to this transformation, she was promoted to team leader in Marketing due to her amazing talent and innovative thinking. However, her relationship issues with her team and supervisors quickly escalated. It is no surprise, then, that this element of being present in relationships with others showed up on the Optimal Being assessment results as her greatest challenge.

The Interview

Welcome Caron! Come on in.

Caron entered and took a seat in a club chair a comfortable distance from mine. A small round table stood between our armrests. She put down her beverage, took a breath, and looked me square in the eye with a twinkle and a smile. She sat easily in the chair—arms unfolded, feet flat on the floor. The first descriptive word that came to my mind was *open* as my gaze landed on her warm, brown eyes. I realized I was already at ease with her.

> I am so happy to be here. Everyone is talking about these interviews, and it is really drumming up curiosity. As I was walking from my desk to here, two people asked me if they could learn what we have all been learning. I love it. I just love it!

I'm thrilled to hear that. And, you are an inspiration to others, especially regarding our topic today. I know you have excelled in a number of elements of well-being. I applaud your commitment to yourself and your teammates. Today, we're going to discuss your number-one challenge at the time you were introduced to the program.

Ethan, let's cut to the chase. I was horrible to people. I was angry. I was judgmental. I was distrustful. I put people in these buckets of horrid categories, and when they were in my space, I strategized to manipulate and move people out of my way. It was second nature. I was not even consciously aware, most of the time, that I was doing anything. I was raised to act this way. I didn't trust anybody.

Let me share an example: I remember waking up one morning when I was a kid, being yelled at by my dad. I felt like the smallest, tiniest ant of a person. I vowed to grow strong enough to never be in that position again. As an adult, I sought out love, but had so much trouble understanding who I truly was and needed to discover who my father was to me. I was playing out dynamics at home and work rooted in that dysfunctional relationship.

I was not a nice, soft, easy person to work with. What really tormented the company was my knack for identifying opportunities where I could look better than others, and then I would manipulate people to support their own destruction. I don't even know if my bosses knew about it, although they will when they see this interview. There were others who were doing the same thing, perhaps following my model. It was not a healthy culture.

I was creating destructive chaos, for sure, for the people I was working with, our clients, and the financial health of Easy Breezy. I was the cause of so much disruption that I'm embarrassed in some ways and so proud in others.

That's an interesting expression. What do you mean, Caron, when you say you were embarrassed and proud?

Well, obviously I'm embarrassed because I can look back on what I did and see it was so hurtful. I know it was hurtful. I am aware now. Why am I proud? I have three children, and I saw how they were copying my behavior, acting it out in school and at home. I changed my patterns and adjusted my parenting, and their behavior transformed. I wouldn't say we're one hundred percent there, but it's night and day from where we were three or four months ago. I'm thankful. I attribute it to changing my patterns, though as you mentioned, I have made strides in a number of areas. However, this one in particular has a way of showing up.

Let's focus on this element, then. Will you tell us about it? What is it exactly?

Okay. It is about what we are like in relationships with others. *Am I able to stay present while someone is triggering my shit?*

It is easy when I am with friends or when my kids are doing what I expect. I can be at peace and life is peachy. But the question is: Can I stay present when the Marketing Director tells me I need to stay late to apply last-minute changes and my nanny—I'm a single mom—needs to leave on time that day? In that moment, am I seeing the good in my boss? How about my nanny? And, what about those kids who are *in my way* for the moment? Sorry, a bit of my dad is coming out.

I noticed Caron's energy had shifted. She had crossed her arms and legs, drawing herself back into her chair. I wondered if a memory of her father triggered the shift. I chose to stay silent as she took a couple of deep breaths, unfolded herself, and continued.

Here it is. You see, before working on this element, I would have thought my boss was an asshole, my nanny was a selfish bitch, and my kids should be able to get along on their own—or just grow up. They are nine, three, and two, by the way.

Caron shrugged and smirked, obviously aware two-year-olds can't take care of themselves.

If I take a moment to see the truth of who they are, I can see my boss is likely getting some pressure from somewhere else and looking for a solution. He has been so supportive in the past and would likely support me again. I needed to be honest with him. And, my nanny loves those kids as if they were her own. She is a beautiful person who, in this example, has a commitment, and I want to be there for her as she has been for me. And, the kids? They are pure love in my life, and as I close my eyes, I remember how beautiful and amazing they are.

Caron actually closed her eyes and did this live, pausing to breathe consciously as her emotions rose to the surface. As a Guide in the Optimal Being program, I was impressed and encouraged at the same time.

Now that I can see what is true about these people, I am able to tell my boss the situation. It doesn't mean I will leave or stay regarding the work, but it does allow for a constructive conversation and better outcome. Letting perceptions of others change takes practice. It's worth it.

What a powerful example of this element in action. What is life like, now that your ability to be present in relationships with others is more of a strength than a weakness?

I can't say that I am seeing each person as *love*, their optimal being, like the course teaches, but I am doing better! I now look for the highest and best in others and realize when I do this, it ends up working out for me too—often in ways I couldn't imagine. I love those types of surprises. I was putting people in these buckets of judgments, and now the buckets are melting away. Oh, and—this is big! I'm allowing myself to see people how they are now and not how they have been.

I'm trusting people more, and I'm more engaged and willing to collaborate. Another new thing: I let others play their part. I used to steal people's opportunities to get more credit. It turns out I wanted recognition to make up for the lack of it growing up. That has all but healed, and I no longer justify hurting others.

Also, I'm having more direct conversations with people. Before, I would let things fester. I used to see conflict as *me versus them*. Now, I understand we all see things through our own history and perception. People aren't *good* when they agree with me nor *bad* when they disagree. I take time to understand why they look at things a certain way. I share my view and together we can communicate and reach the best outcome.

I'm able to be present with other people as I am. No judgments. No guardedness or pretense. I now feel joy most of the time when I am with others.

Caron, this is so good. I can see your face glowing as you talk. Wow! Is there anything that surfaced through the process that was a big aha! moment for you beyond what you have shared already?

Yes. I hated myself for something I didn't know I hated myself for. That showed up as hate for others, but the source was in me. Once I realized this, I allowed myself to experience the hate and actually seek it out. I opened up to my feelings and asked the hate why it existed.

My curiosity was piqued. I found myself eager to learn what Caron had discovered.

So, did you come up with any insights?

Well, I would say I have, but I might be addressing some of what Roma will be sharing with you in your next interview. I saw her name on the schedule.

How about just sharing the highlights?

Sure. I used to need pain in order to get attention, and I confused this for love. I don't do that any longer. I now see that pain is pain, there to reveal whatever I need to know. I needed attention because I had rejected myself and the part of me that was clear about my purpose.

Caron once again drew a deep, steadying breath.

Hate was a process that allowed me to see that I had rejected myself. It was a message from me to see the rejection and make a new choice. Once I listened to the hate and was able to *be with it*, I heard in my heart what to do. It won't be the same for everyone, perhaps, but I was led to pray. My resistance left me, and relief washed over me like warm water. I then looked in the mirror and saw myself as the loving being I am. It was spectacular. I feel it now, as we are talking. I truly accept who I am, and that helped me accept others. You are smiling! You have heard this from others?

I have. I never grow tired of hearing it. I am curious about the prayer. Is there anything you are willing to share about it? Is it a prayer that may serve others?

Yes, of course. I know exactly what it was and have offered it to friends. It goes like this:

> *I am done hating myself.*
> *I am worthy of love.*
> *I am ready to live in alignment with my best self.*
> *I accept myself.*
> *I accept myself.*
> *I accept myself.*

The words just poured out of me. I spoke them, but it was like they came through me rather than from me. A previously inaccessible *somewhere* in me opened, and out came wisdom and love.

Caron, you have shown healthy relationships are possible for anyone. You also showed how healing is possible, even for the distant past. Thank you so much. I know it's not always easy to make these changes if people in your life believe what they want to believe about you. How do others know your changes are authentic and not just part of a new manipulation?

> It's interesting that you bring that up. I am still working on accepting that it's okay when people perceive me how they do. Some people will keep me in their *bucket* of manipulative people, but I am doing my best to let them have that opinion while being the authentic me. I trust more people will see the *new me*, the real me, over time, but I have a history of creating disorder and distrust at work. There will be cynics with closed minds about me. It's up to me to be consistent with this, and if anything needs to be addressed, I will do my best to act with courage and start an open conversation. I've learned to ask for support. Sometimes, support comes from the person I have the greatest conflict with. That's been a real eye-opener for me.

Awesome. Beautiful. Thank you, thank you, thank you, Caron. Please contact me if you have additional thoughts you would like to include, Okay? Also, when you leave, please let Roma know I need a few minutes.

> Okay, great, thank you so much.

Interview Notes

Some of the things Caron shared may not relate exactly to you, but we can all recall a person who creates drama wherever they go.

I was impressed with the way she has put this element into concrete action. She is transforming into the best version of herself. The benefits of her transformation have proven immeasurable for her team. Caron's honesty and openness are refreshing. It's not easy to be as vulnerable as she was without being truly committed to treating others well.

It is one thing to be in your optimal state when thinking about or in the presence of others, but the next element will take this even closer to home, when we look further at maintaining your optimal being in relationship with yourself.

The Well-Being Element of Maintaining Optimal Being (Love) in the Presence of Others

There are certain characteristics that leaders want in employees, and a global survey revealed the number-two characteristic of a *problem* employee is someone who can't work well with others.[6] However, when a manager exemplifies this well-being element, they treat employees more humanely, they listen, they're attentive, and they are more conscientious. Since employees who feel heard are 460 percent more likely to feel empowered to perform their best, this is a *big* one![7]

This element significantly impacts an organization. Consider that 58 percent of people say they trust strangers more than their boss. Translation: Critical human relations are not present in six out of ten relationships with bosses. Distrust amplifies issues across any company, leading to high levels of disengagement and dissatisfaction, undermining what is possible for a workforce.

Shifting this element in your organization has so many benefits. See more about how it plays out personally and organizationally as a challenge or when optimal by scanning this QR code with your phone's camera.

QR code URL: optimalbeing.live/well-being-info-graphic

Chapter 4

Roma: Relationship With Self

Roma, in modern Italian usage, means *a beautiful woman*— inside and out.

Roma works on a production line for Easy Breezy, creating the products it provides to customers. I paused to silently express gratitude for her participation in Optimal Being as she swept into the room.

The Interview

Hey, Roma, come on in.

Roma brought the sunshine with her. Her golden yellow blouse and springy step resonated a smile in me. Caron was glowing after the last interview, and Roma was radiant on her way in. She took a seat.

So great to see you. How are you today, Roma?

> I feel so much joy, and a lot of appreciation for feeling happy.

This was not always true?

> I used to be so mean to myself. I really thought I was worthless. It was as if I were an apple tree and hated myself for not producing better pears. Now, I see how amazing it is to be an apple tree, and I'm discovering how much I had denied about myself.

Let's start with an exercise from the Optimal Being program. Tell me something you discovered you love about yourself.

> Sure, that's an easy one. I am a happy person, and I light up the room when I enter it—no matter who's there. Before, I would be the one hiding if certain people were in the room. I was intimidated, feeling I didn't measure up to people who were cool and confident— for example, strong people and leaders who were highly respected. Their presence pushed my intimidation

buttons. I wouldn't let my personality, my light, shine, so I hid as best I could.

No more. I have every right to let my best self show up just as they do. Now, instead of comparing myself to them, an awful habit, I show up like this, as I am. I'm amazed at how easy it's becoming. My envy has gone from green to white, shining my light instead of wanting theirs.

That's so good to hear. Tell me a little bit more about where you were before, regarding this third element of being the expression of love that you are.

Okay. Well, the third element is really about my relationship with myself. How I treat myself, what my self-talk says, and my feelings when I think about me. This covers the current moment and when I think about me in the past or future. I have not always been able to see myself clearly when I thought about the future. I was full of horrible self-judgment for so many years. Even though I'm really bright and pretty well-liked, I didn't always see it that way.

If I made a mistake, I would tear into myself. I would dwell on how I upset somebody, how foolish I looked. I always believed I'd missed out on an opportunity to be great.

I was such a people pleaser, totally insecure. I sought out people to lift me up, constantly seeking help so no one could see how bad I was. It's like I was raising my hand saying, "Please pick me or join me or rescue me." I was terrified. I was an energy drainer with anybody in the office who cared enough to *help me*. They would do their best, but they only helped me short term, and I could be exhausting. I burned some people out and noticed when they wanted to pull away. However, I was still stuck with myself at the end of the day.

And . . .

Something had to change, Ethan. I needed to shift the way I thought about myself. I had to find a way to end the inner spinning that just would not quit. Thankfully, I learned how to interrupt the internal critic and self-talk. Instead of pushing it away, I now look forward to it and embrace it.

Excuse me, Roma. Did you say "look forward" to your inner critic?

Yes. I know it may sound strange, but each thought brings information. *You're ugly* was a message I believed about myself, and it showed up for twenty years. Arguing with it seemed to make it stronger and meaner. When I listened to my inner critic and appreciated it, the opposite thing happened. The hateful talk went away. It now says how beautiful I am inside and out. I love it.

It went away and now says nice things? I'd love to hear more about that.

Yes. It took a while. There was a lot in there, but yes, I listened, and the energy changed from attack to support. The messages changed. The emotional charge changed. I see this, and so many other things, as *healed parts of myself.*

Amazing. Is this lesson something you are willing to share? There are a lot of inner critics out there who could benefit from your story.

Of course, it was something I learned during an Optimal Being group mentoring session. Shortly after, I was going for a walk, and my inner critic started pointing out how stupid I was. It said I was ugly and I needed to go hide myself. I looked down. I was wearing an old pair of sweatpants and a raggedy shirt. I laughed. "Thanks for pointing out the obvious," I said out loud to myself.

"You have always been ugly," that voice said.

I was connecting breaths and allowing my feelings— practices from our program—so I was calm as this conversation started, but it was obvious the energy was amping up. "Thank you. Anything else?" I replied, taking the time I needed to breathe and feel.

"Yeah, you have ugly children too," the voice challenged me. That one was a bit more confronting, but I breathed and felt the energy in me change.

"Thank you," I replied with a smile. "Is there anything else?"

This went on for a twenty-minute walk, and we finally arrived at the end of the insults. I asked if there was anything more and it said, "Yes. You are really quite beautiful."

I said thank you and asked if there was anything more.

The voice said, "No. I've said everything I want to say."

I replied, "Thank you, and who are you?"

"I am you."

I then asked why I was saying those things to myself, and I heard, "You judged yourself as ugly after your first child twenty years ago and compared yourself to how you were before having children. You never felt pretty enough. You hung on to the old and called the changes in you *ugly*."

I started crying because I knew it was right. I was right and I never saw it. I had missed it for twenty years. But, I accept myself now. I see the awesome gift of my children, and I feel blessed in my body, exactly as it is. By the way, once I accepted me, I was inspired to change a few things.

The excess weight is disappearing too. It's fine on me and it's fine off. I like me either way now, but I do have a preference.

That sounds pretty advanced. How long did it take you to have this experience?

I was about four weeks into the program. I had been practicing one of the strategies in my assessment results:

1. Stop
2. Interrupt the voice
3. Reset into an aligned place with love
4. Allow my thoughts to come forward from that loving place rather than from anger, hurt, and hate

Then someone brought it up in the group meeting, and I practiced and practiced and allowed my thoughts to come forward from that loving place rather than from anger, hurt, and hate. It's been several months now, and I've had other messages come to me—it's pretty much the same process over and over with a few variations. Change can be good, really good.

I like myself, and instead of seeking validation from outside, I found new ways of supporting myself from the inside. The shift has really changed everything.

Guess what? My doctor is lowering my prescriptions after my lab tests and says I may no longer need the medications at all in six to eight months. Either way, there's a level of health showing up as I surrender judgments about myself.

As I practiced the love exchange process from the program—where I look in a mirror and extend love to myself—the changes sped up. Every week, I read the commitment letter to myself from the Optimal Being app. It reminds me of my worth, so I'm willing to honor myself as I am. I am enough, and what I *do* is no longer my source of self-worth.

I know it doesn't determine your value as a person, but have you had any changes in what you are doing in your life, Roma?

Instead of trying to overcome all my weaknesses, I have brought out more of my strengths. Instead of trying to do things I'm not great at to prove myself worthy, I focus on areas where I am interested and strong. I don't chase my weaknesses; I make room for people who are exceptional in those areas to shine. Everything works out better. I've even put my application in to be a line lead. It will be a stretch, but long-term, I believe I'll be great in that role.

I'm sure you will! Excellent, how else?

Regarding doing? Hmmm. A real win is that I'm not drawing on the energy of others. That has basically stopped. Incredibly, I actually had to ask the people who were playing out my old habits with me to stop trying to help. I met with each person and said, "Look, I know in the past I've been really needy. I've not been happy. I didn't like myself very much, and you've done a lot to support me when I came to you, often desperate. From now on, anytime you notice me falling back into that old pattern, I give you permission to hand me one of these cards.

I gave each of them a number of cards that had printed on them:

> I am all that I am.
>
> What's one thing I love about myself, something I cherish about me?
>
> Ask whoever gave me this card what they love and cherish about me.
>
> Listen to them, and believe they are being honest.

I finished by telling them, "If I ever ask for more than normal support at work, please hand me this card."

That created a healthy boundary. This little, simple thing has worked miracles with those people. I've been able to learn about them, instead of having all the focus on helping me. I've been able to enjoy them.

I would tell anybody who feels worthless, insecure, and is full of negative self-talk to recognize that you can change all of it. You can see the love and beauty in yourself and stop the hating and self-abuse. Those voice in your head are gifts, exposing beliefs and content, even if untrue. Listening to what is there with no judgment can lead to messages being revealed that are important for your restoration. It is possible for anything false to fail and truth to prevail.

So well said, Roma. What about family?

You know what? I had a moment with my mom that blew my mind. Remember the critic and *you're ugly* conversation? Well, I shared that healing story with my mom, and she gasped and cried. She had that critic in her too. As we talked about it, we realized it likely went back to my great-great-grandmother, who had a deformity in her face. So, I taught my mom to talk with her critic, and use the tools I learned. She has always been a beautiful person, but now she, too, sees her beauty.

Oh, I just love it!

Roma raised her arms up as if she'd just won the *Tour De France*. I raised my arms with her in celebration.

Thank you, Roma. You're such a blessing. We appreciate you and thank you for being so open and vulnerable in sharing some of these wounds and the restoration of such a beautiful human being. You know so many see you as a beacon of light, and I look forward to hearing your continued progress.

Roma gave me thumbs up as she rose and walked out the door.

Interview Notes

Roma is a line worker, a person who could easily be *invisible* in a company this size. Now that she knows her worth and strengths, she does not need to hide in order to avoid the spotlight of responsibility. Roma is honest about her strengths and gifts and acknowledges areas that are a challenge for her. This attribute will make her an effective leader, bringing out the strength in others.

The Well-Being Element of Being Present With Self

Roma mentioned reading the *Commitment to Self* letter. The Optimal Being program includes a commitment letter for several situations in an app, which is free to anyone right now for any device via Apple and Google Play. The commitment letters have decades of history and countless testimonials about how powerful changes come from the words we speak. By simply reading and speaking these words regularly, change occurs in relationships with self and others.

Roma's story also shows us that being present as our optimal being (love) in the presence of self improves physical and mental health. Since 66 percent of employees report experiencing symptoms of depression at least sometimes,[8] and the numbers are growing, mastering this one element of well-being can be a lifesaver.

Shifting this element in your organization has so many benefits. See more about how it plays out personally and organizationally as a challenge or when optimal by scanning this QR code with your phone's camera.

QR code URL: optimalbeing.live/well-being-info-graphic

Chapter 5

Alethia: Relationship With Truth

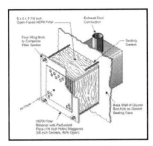

From DOE Nuclear Air Cleaning Handbook[9]

Alethia chose her name after a Greek goddess, and it means *truth* or *disclosure*. Her downfall exhibited quite the opposite.

When I first met Alethia, she was struggling. In the midst of a lawsuit, her heels were dug in, and I was not well received. Her demeanor was unpleasant. Alethia resisted people who opposed her, and anyone who dared challenge her was considered her enemy. She was closed to working with Optimal Being at first as she didn't think it was for her. After all, Alethia knew what was right and had mastered defending her position.

People with fixed, rigid mindsets like Alethia's can be difficult to be around because they know what they know and have convinced themselves they are right. They believe what they say, even when it is untrue. They typically push away the truth, often unaware they are doing it. Don't tell them though, or you will have pulled out a knife at a gun fight *(Thank you, Indiana Jones)*. I was interested to learn how the program affected Alethia and her role as Director of Manufacturing Operations, especially as the Truth element was her number-one challenge.

The Interview

Alethia entered wearing a red dress and tall black boots. Her demeanor was all business. She quickly sat and placed her small purse on the floor, propped a notebook on her right thigh, and, pen in hand, crossed over her left leg.

Let's get started.

Okay. Yeah, let's get started. Alethia, why don't . . . Actually, where would you like to start?

She smiled in appreciation.

Well, I'll tell you a story about what my life was like before I became aware the well-being element of Truth was an issue for me. I believed I was right, and if you tried to present anything that conflicted with my "rightness," I poo-pooed it. I would perhaps feign listening, but I was rarely able to actually listen. It became apparent early on, when going through the training in these elements, that this was an issue for me, but I didn't want anyone to know. So, I did my best to work on this in secret. That may have been a mistake in terms of how quickly I could have made progress, but it was the way I did it. You and I met at the height of my denial. You'll appreciate this story.

One day, my team brought me a customer claim stating our new filters arrived but were unusable. I was appalled because I personally had inspected the test data and the product before shipping. If there was actually a problem, it would have exposed me and others as incompetent, and it would have been costly. I dismissed the customer's feedback and decided they made up a story to negotiate.

After burying the input, we packaged up another ten thousand units and distributed them to retailers across the world. The challenge appeared again, this time as a lawsuit from a major customer for the same defect. The issue, a leaky seal produced in the packaging process, allowed moisture to enter and contaminate the product, essentially making it worthless.

Instead of admitting the truth and addressing it, I denied any previous knowledge as we went into legal proceedings. You and I met at the tail end of that. I was in my full stress response at that time. My pulse and blood pressure were elevated, my skin was flushed, my mind spun, and my head felt like it might explode. I now call it my *how dare you tell me the truth* state.

Meanwhile, we were in the process of recalling the units, discarding the old, and replacing them with products that worked. It turned out the actual problem with the seal was easily rectified. If only I had listened! Ugh.

Our head of production ratted me out in his deposition. I was furious. He should have had my back. Remember, this was when acknowledging the Truth was my biggest well-being issue. Suddenly, my job was in jeopardy, and my team felt betrayed as I failed to pass on the original customers' complaint they had brought me. Uncomfortable to admit, but true.

I've learned, through doing the exercises in the program, that I refused to hear the truth because it reminded me of all the times I felt embarrassment for being inaccurate or wrong in school. I still recall my third-grade teacher publicly humiliating me for how stupid I was because I couldn't explain a math problem.

Suddenly, I remembered a detail from her personnel file.

Wait, Alethia, weren't you a math major in college?

Yes, and it was probably because of this third-grade situation. When it happened, I thought, "I never want to feel like this this again." How did I feel? Physically, my face felt tense and hot. It must have looked beet red, and I thought my head might explode. Sound familiar? I was humiliated and embarrassed and told my mind and body to protect me from those feelings and experiences.

I finally grasped this after an Optimal Being Facilitator convinced me I had a truth challenge. I didn't believe it at first. I then remembered this embarrassment and allowed the actual truth to surface. It turned out this third-grade event was reinforced over many years. Different people, same dynamic. As soon as I sensed I'd done something wrong, I would do anything and everything to prevent exposure.

Honestly, I often pretended I knew stuff when I didn't. Then I'd defend my position even though others could tell I was making it up on the fly. After a while, I became a great liar—to myself and others. The truth was somewhere in me, but it brought up too much pain for me to accept.

Here's the problem—lying doesn't work. Things ended in disaster too many times to count because I didn't know what I was doing and wouldn't admit it. The largest and latest disaster: thousands of units recalled and a lawsuit that cost our company dearly in time, money, reputation—and almost cost me my job.

If you could learn from your history, do you have any insight into how you might handle that same situation today?

I have thought about it. Today, I am confident I would look at the production facility immediately and stop the line. Upon inquiry, the issue and its correction would surface and be resolved. I would feel gratitude and call to celebrate the client who brought it to our attention. I'd feel a bit like Oprah; wins for everyone. *You get a win! And you get a win!*

Alethia laughed and began ticking off items on her fingers.

Recall averted. Customer relationship advanced. Team validated for bringing it to my attention. And me? I'd be the person who saved, not cost, the company a ton of money, even if no one knew it.

I had so many moments when I could have listened and disclosed the truth. Unfortunately, I was unwilling to feel the pain that would have come with it.

She paused and was clearly thinking a new thought for her. Her eyes squinted just a bit before she spoke.

I remember hearing "the truth hurts" when I was a kid, and thought truth was a thing to avoid. However, anyone denying the truth will inevitably feel the pain their lie was trying to suppress. Willingness to feel that pain is actually something to embrace. The truth brings life after a nanosecond of pain. The truth really hurts when we hide it behind a lie we try to keep alive.

Wow, did that just come out of my mouth? That was good!

A remarkable statement, Alethia. The longer we keep a lie, the more painful the truth will appear. I'm now curious, what else has been affected by addressing this issue?

Relationships. Before, I was rigid in my thinking and argued when someone didn't agree with me, or I just dismissed them. You know that leadership survey you shared with our team that describes problem employees?

I nodded.

The Center for Creative Leadership cites the fourth of eleven characteristics common in problem employees is resistance to change.[10] I epitomized this.

She pointed to her chest as she said the final sentence, and then, she grew quiet and seemed to daydream, looking off into space. After a deep breath, she came back with a sigh.

I had a recent phone call from a major producer talking about a shift in our industry. I noticed my resistance and my blood pressure rising, reminding me I didn't like change. I told myself to let go of being right and to release trying to defend our current strategy. After the call, I gave myself permission to sit for fifteen minutes and look at my notes.

As I did, I noticed tremendous heat flowing through me as tension grew in my body. I caught myself holding my breath, so I relaxed into conscious breathing—like I learned in the program. I realized I wanted these notes to be different than they were. But the words stayed the same, and the producer's voice echoed in my head. I finally accepted that it was as it was. Ignoring it was not an option—not this time.

Within a minute or two, I had an inspired thought: We could adapt our current production to incorporate this industry shift. There could even be a profitability surge if we embraced this innovation, rather than trying to hold on to our tried-and-*true* methods.

I had an aha! moment. It was worth feeling discomfort for a few minutes as I listened and let go of attachment to our current way of doing things. I had fought hard for our strategy just a few weeks earlier, so the initial thought of presenting this change to the board felt like failure. I imagined me standing there looking stupid, just like in the third grade. But, after my emotions surfaced and I allowed myself to shift, I realized the board at Easy Breezy would want me to make the choice I was making.

True story. I was embraced for being flexible and for moving on this so quickly.

Nice! That must feel so good. Alethia, what would you say to someone who is questioning whether they can benefit from making these elements of well-being a priority in their workforce?

She listened to the question and looked me square in the eyes. I realized I was experiencing Alethia as a company leader, an awakened leader. I leaned forward, actively listening to every word.

First, until we're open to what actually is, rather than what we want things to be, we are denying the truth. When we accept this, it helps us see more of what actually is true. We see more of the available information and can make better choices. For example, if you are convinced there are only three TV stations, you will jump from one to two to three and miss the hundreds out there. Hanging on to the idea there are only three does not make it true.

Many leaders are zeroed in on *channels* they grew up with in business. Profit. Process. Innovation. People, etc. There is another channel called *well-being*, and it has become a *top* channel in our business. Get that right, and it's like the other channels jump from rabbit-ears technology to HD.

As leaders, the effect of our well-being is magnified by our influence in the organization. Have we awakened the optimal leader within us? Once we are awakened to this, we refine it until we can sustain that optimal state of *being* consistently. I am learning still—with room for massive improvement.

Ethan, I am enjoying the process so much, but not just at work.

I've seen this play out in a really powerful way at home, too, particularly discussing politics. I'm a Democrat and my husband leans Republican. We were so rigid in our positions; we couldn't hear each other. Now, we are open instead of defensive. We even read and watch news on both sides. While doing this, it has become rather obvious how misleading both sides can be at times, and we have since found sources more even in their reporting. It's been fun.

By practicing with politics at home, I've grown more sensitive to sensations which seem to be indicating: *Something is off! Open. Relax. Listen.* Before, I thought my feelings were telling me: *Shut it down. This is not right. Too much distress.*

Now, I recognize how my feelings support my becoming aware. I've learned to ask: *Anything to be aware of? I'm open.* Then, I breathe, feel, and pay attention. Sometimes the message will come to me as a thought and others, an action. Memories sometimes surface and often an insight will come perfect for the moment. I always ask, "anything else?" until it is clear the message is fully received.

Just-in-time insights, like your near-catastrophe at the coffee shop? Yes, I heard about that.

Oh my gosh, yes. Do we have time to for me to share it?

Of course . . .

Okay. One day I parked and walked toward my favorite coffee shop. On my way in, I felt a strong sensation. Nothing appeared unusual, but it was a clear interruption to my flow that morning. At first, I resisted it and said to myself: *I'll just get my coffee, get back in my car, and head to the office.* But, as I got closer to the door, the sensation grew. It was like my sixth sense kicked in, and I knew not to go into that shop.

So, I paused, took a breath, and moved to the side. I was confused as I wandered back to my car, even a bit upset that I was being guided from within *not* to get my coffee. Just then, a vehicle lost control, bounced over the curb and crashed right into the coffee shop's entrance. Ethan, I literally would have been standing where the car came to a rest. I was honestly mortified at first—then awestricken and thankful.

If there had been a question before as to whether information is available beyond the five physical senses, it no longer was a question. In that moment, I realized the guidance system you talk about is not only real, but even beyond what I thought possible. Yet, if you ask around our company, you will hear story after story highlighting similar extraordinary moments, though no other cars in coffee shops.

Consistently, I get insights and trust them more and more, even when no supporting evidence warrants trusting them in the outside world. That inner source has become credible with me, and when I join with others who are *in-tune* with their Optimal Being, it's remarkable. So, even though I gave a bunch of examples of how it's important to listen to other people and outside information, it's just as powerful to recognize the insights coming from within.

I don't even know if you want to include this in the interview, as it may sound *out there* to some people, but I hope you do. This guidance is available.

I have goose bumps. Sharing that is a brave thing, Alethia, as not everyone will have a personal experience they can relate to. I will confess your description matches the experiences I hear from others as well as my own.

Before we wrap up, is there anything else you feel inspired to share?

Yes, just one more thing. My daughter. She has been using some of the tools your company teaches too. She is more willing to see the truth even if she feels discomfort. The cascading effect serves our family in a really cool way.

Sadly, she was convinced I was a loser, and concluded she must be a loser too. With hope dwindling, she was angry and hurting. In an effort to open things up at home, my husband and I created a game called *Beat the Loser*. It was a card game, and whoever lost was *beaten* with a blow-up porcupine doll.

One night she was laughing and crying as I was in the *loser* seat, and her arms flailed with delight and her hair swung from side to side as she hit me. She finished and said, "You know what, I had a thought. What if I'm wrong about you being a loser? You are all right, Mom." She swung those arms around my me as I sat in that chair, and I just cried and cried. So did she. Everything seemed to change for her after that.

I smiled at her, taking in how incredible that must be for Alethia, her daughter, and their family. The interview came to an end and we stood to say goodbye.

Thank you, Alethia. As you go out, would you please invite Jabari in. I'm talking with him about fearlessness.

Oh my! I saw the changes in Jabari as we went through the program together. What a transformation! He shared a number of his successes in our group mentoring sessions, and I saw his confidence rise throughout the weeks.

Interview Notes

I marveled at my conversation with Alethia. Her personal journey is influencing positive change in so many areas: leadership, her team members, client relations, her marriage, and their daughter. She exemplifies so many possibilities available to organizations who seek to support and awaken their optimal workforces.

Personally, I was grateful for the shifts in my own perceptions of Alethia as our past encounter had been difficult. I experienced gratitude for her growth and for my own.

The Well-Being Element of Being Present with Truth

There are many reasons truth might be hidden. Guilt, shame, fear, insecurity, sadness, anger, and more are tucked away and ready to surface with the truth. Memories we want to forget may surface with the truth. Strategies to protect us and keep us safe from feeling pain can also block or prevent us from seeing the truth. Defending our positions and needing to be right are common when this is a challenge.

When we block truth at work, issues mount. We avoid the conversations that could bring resolution. We blur our receptivity to insights. We lose opportunities. Blocked truth can lead to the loss of key employees, missed sales, and dysfunctional patterns against the organization's best interests, including the realization of its mission, objectives, and vision.

As a strength, this element of well-being can lead to focus and clear direction and quicken goal achievement.

A study by Richard Hunsaker shows how big an issue this truth challenge is by measuring ineffective listening, just one strategy to block the truth. He cites 75 percent of the time employees are distracted, preoccupied, or forgetful when listening.[11]

Wouldn't we all prefer honesty, open-mindedness, and willingness to truly listen? Wouldn't we all love to see rigidity fall away and more true harmony flow at work?

Shifting this element in your organization has so many benefits. See more about how it plays out personally and organizationally as a challenge or as an optimal condition by scanning this QR code with your phone's camera.

QR code URL: optimalbeing.live/well-being-info-graphic

Chapter 6

Jabari: Freedom From Fear

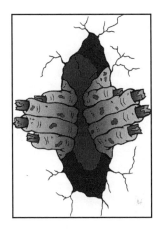

Jabari is Swahili for *brave*.

I noted that Jabari, a Technical Project Manager, shared he had taken a medical leave of absence just prior to the Optimal Being program. He also worked with several Optimal Being Mentors during the process, benefiting significantly from private sessions Easy Breezy offered to employees upon request. I so looked forward to his contribution.

The Interview

Jabari entered with a quick step and a smile. He was casually dressed in stylish jeans and a slick, white button-down shirt, untucked and covered in elaborate white stitching. His light brown skin showed off the shirt's contrast, and his red-framed glasses highlighted a joyful, life-filled face.

He spoke first, with a subtle hint of a Jamaican accent.

Hey, thanks for having me. I appreciate this opportunity.

Jabari, welcome. You're going to share how you went from being fearful to becoming comfortable with fear, and, in some respects, free of fear.

Ah yes, of course.

What does all that mean?

There are many people who experience overwhelming fears. My fear was about being inadequate, not good enough, failing, and not knowing how to handle situations. I didn't trust myself and was not equipped to change that. My strategy was to hide, distract myself, and bury my fear. It was fine when I was a kid. However, it was quite harmful as an adult. What a mess.

He looked down and shook his head. I could sense his discomfort.

Share only what you choose, Jabari. We can skip the details if you prefer.

> No. I want to, if it might help just one person. It is important for me to share my history to let people know it is possible to overcome any fear.

Guides in the Optimal Being program are trained to support others through discomfort, while allowing them to share what they desire. I leaned forward, giving Jabari my full and present attention. Looking him in the eyes, I expressed my appreciation.

Thank you for your courage. I admire what you are doing here. Is there anything you want people to know before you start sharing? Anything that might help them feel more comfortable with your story?

> Yes. This may not ever happen for you, and you might think some of it is crazy. However, this actually happened, and I came out okay. I am healthy now and understand and appreciate why fear is in my life. I now choose to use fear for the positive, not the negative.

> As a child, I saw my dad hit our dog, and feared I might be beaten too. Then one day, my dad did strike me. I was thinking: *Dad must really hate me. If Dad hates me, then I must be unlovable.* I was hurt and began to hate myself. I turned my self-hatred on a friend in a horrible way, leading to unbearable shame.

The shame suppressed deep inside was the direct result of how much I hated myself. Anger came next as thoughts surfaced of being punished by God for being so bad. Wanting to be good enough to be loved by God, I tried to be like Jesus. When I failed at being as good as Jesus, I assumed I would go to hell.

I didn't really believe hell existed as a place. I thought that hell might just be right here on Earth with all the pain that goes with it. Earth was a place where people were hurting and where people hurt each other, and I blamed God for that.

I wanted to be good, to be loved; desperate for someone to tell me I was okay. I was trying to be perfect and had never come close. I wanted to find comfort, though I was never able to shake the feeling that I failed to live up to expectations. In my own eyes, I failed again and again and again.

For many years, I went through ups and downs but came out on top. However, when the promotion I had worked two years to earn finally arrived, I did not experience the feeling of freedom expected. My conclusion: *I must not be good at life.*

Next came a psychotic break. A battle in my mind took over my life. It was ugly for my wife and kids. I felt ashamed later for the pain inflicted, but in the moment of psychosis, I was in awe of what appeared to be transpiring. Though I hadn't done drugs, it reminded me of stories people described of their mind-bending trips. Despite great support from the medical community, I was not feeling like myself. Fears still haunted me.

In this program, I learned that our fears will eventually surface and will always be reflected or mirrored back to us by the world. It is just a matter of when and how. The fear will present itself as a subtle interruption of peace in the beginning. If ignored or pushed away, it will show up again and again, always finding a way to show us what is unsettled, or unresolved in us.

If fear could talk, the message for me is: *You have lots of monsters in your mind and would be happier if you face them and hear what they have to say.*

Monsters? What kind of monsters?

Thoughts, pictures, judgments, and pain I had not wanted to see. I feared that I couldn't handle them, feeling overwhelmed, incapable and unwilling to get help. It sucked.

The four-letter *F*-word to me was F E A R before I was introduced to Optimal Being. I had just left the hospital, was in treatment, and on several medications. The Optimal Being program was not on my to-do list before the hospitalization, but something spoke to me after. Though tempted to ignore the impulse, I needed what that program offered.

Before starting, I requested a private session with one of the facilitators, and it opened my mind to the possibility that I could face the fears and benefit. Most people would not understand the contrast of peace I felt in a short time. It was like going from the bathroom horror scene in *The Shining*, when Jack Nicholson axes through the door, sending shivers through our spines with "Heeeere's Johnny!" to the peace and calm one may feel in nature or with a trusted friend.

But how? How did you feel that peace and what happened to fear?

I would like to say it was easy, but it was not. The tools are simple but applying them again and again took discipline. It was worth the commitment. I learned a process to become aware of fear before it got out of control. I noticed when fear would show up in my breathing, I'd hold my breath. Then, my pulse would race, my muscles would tense up in my neck and I'd feel hot. So, I learned to recognize these signs of fear, feel what I felt, and breathe consciously. My system would invariably relax, and I became aware of what was causing the fear or triggering it.

As you know, Ethan, we call this *being present* in the experience of my fear and trusting I would be okay. I listened to the facilitator and did this again and again, even with thoughts and images in my mind.

Often, another emotion surfaced after the fear dissolved, and I would follow the process with those feelings, too. I learned to be okay with just about anything that arose in my mind or in my body. There were moments I needed support. For those moments, I called my wife, or a coworker, and occasionally, reached out directly to one of the Optimal Being Mentors. Some of the time, I could do it on my own, and today, that is true more often than not. I now trust and can be present in 90-plus percent of the situations when fears surface.

I know fear will show up again, and will embrace it instead of brushing it aside, running from it, or trying to escape its hold on me. Now, I can honestly say I often welcome fear as an opportunity, for sure.

Jabari smiled. Then, he laughed and said,

Wow, didn't know I would be sharing all of that!

I'm glad you did, Jabari. I am learning here too. What is different for you at work, now that you have more confidence to face fear directly when it shows up?

Before, I believed people were out to get me, and was afraid of feeling embarrassment; on alert for any person who could put my reputation at risk. I needed to be seen as *great at my job* and took as much credit as I could because *credit* meant I was good. I loved when people praised me and said my work was exceptional. I was a taker in that regard.

I'm aware of my old habits. It is optimal for me to feel any emotion surfacing in me when I am around people who appear to pose a *threat*. I say *threat* because it's the perception of a threat that triggers feelings I didn't want to feel. I am still retraining my system, but now, I accept my feelings as being related to past patterns and ask for love to guide me to heal. Inspired guidance invariably shows up. This helps me be more present in the moment with people—even those I thought were a *threat*.

For example, my boss asked if I would go on stage and tell my story of how my insanity turned out to be a gift. Speaking about my issue would have really upset me before. Instead, I felt honored to be asked and had no emotional charges about sharing something that many people would keep secret if possible. Shortly thereafter, I was asked to be part of your interview about the fear element of well-being.

I now see fear as a gift, telling me something. Instead of running and hiding from it, I feel it and stay open to see what it is revealing. That is the benefit of this being a strength. Everything feels easy in comparison to what I used to do.

Jabari, words cannot describe how transformative your interview will be for so many. The last question I have is whether you have any other ideas, tips, tricks, or support for people who struggle with fear as a top issue in their lives.

> *As it is outside, it is inside.* If you are experiencing fear in your life, you are projecting that fear on the world. If you want your outer world to change, go and face your fears. Does that mean things that used to bring out your fear will disappear? Not always. Murder, hate, job challenges, rejection, harassment—all these things still exist, but how you experience them in the world will change.
>
> I marvel at how peaceful my life has become while the world appears chaotic. I am centered and in harmony. This arrived by facing the hidden realities in me.
>
> Hope that helps, Ethan.

Those are all my questions today. I wonder if you could stay a bit after we turn off the camera.

Interview Notes

After the interview was completed, I told Jabari a fear had surfaced during his interview and asked if he would support me in processing it. He did, of course, leaning forward and giving me his full attention. I shared this story:

When I was five years old, I feared a monster coming up from the toilet and grabbing me and taking me away. I used to ask for someone to go to the bathroom with me. I hated it and felt embarrassed. So I crossed my legs and tried to hold it in as long as I could. This pain is still real for me as an adult. It no longer shows up in the bathroom, but does show up as fears of unseen threats, much like you had faced. It affected me at work when I withdrew at times when I needed to persist.

Jabari supported me in a stellar way as I walked through some of the tools we both had learned to embrace: connecting my breath, feeling emotions, allowing ideas and memory to surface, and inviting love to restore me and correct my perceptions. I discovered I was afraid of being punished and even more afraid of my thoughts of retaliation for that punishment.

I appreciated him so much for that moment. Asking Jabari for support helped me reveal an insight much needed for me, and I loved that he was the teacher and I became the student. I was reminded it is okay to face things no matter what our age or when an incident takes place. I felt the healing in my body, mind, spirit, and emotions immediately.

Jabari faced his fear, and he is an example of someone who is now more able to create the life he wants. He is happier and more able to accomplish what he desires. If you share this challenge with Jabari, hang in there because you, too, can experience freedom from fear. Addressing this element—

and others—requires undoing some of the patterns you have through two approaches: education and application. In the Optimal Being program, participants first learn principles of the program. Then, they apply these principles through well-designed, tried-and-true tools in regular practice. Over time, many of the practices become habits, or, as Jabari said, they become *easier and easier* to incorporate into a life of optimal being.

We will learn in the next well-being element how hostility can be addressed and shift patterns that may be lifelong, engrained patterns of destruction. Ping's story is worth hearing. Even if you are not dealing with anger as an issue, odds are high that you know someone who has this challenge.

The Well-Being Element of Freedom From Fear

One-third of the workforce is afraid of losing their job, two-thirds fear being undercompensated, and one-third fears discrimination.[12] Those are just a few of the fears present in our daily places of work. Many, in the same study by Chapman University, fear bullying, sexual harassment, and physical assault.

Because fear will always lead to negative outcomes, using it to motivate yourself or others, hiding it, and acting from it will not serve anyone. This must be a mastered concept if you want to excel in your life. It is something you absolutely can master. In the Optimal Being program, you learn tools to embrace fear and to shift that negative energy into an energy or force of power and strength rooted in love.

In our general culture, fear is now being seeded and harvested as a commodity. Fear is easily used to manipulate behavior, promote purchasing, or even persuade people to believe a particular version of a story. This fear does not serve us, either, and we can learn to recognize when others are cultivating our fear—and move beyond their efforts.

Shifting this element in your organization has so many benefits. See more about how it plays out personally and organizationally as a challenge or when optimal by scanning this QR code with your phone's camera.

QR code URL: optimalbeing.live/well-being-info-graphic

Chapter 7

Ping: Freedom From Anger and Hostility

Ping means *even* or *peaceful* in Chinese.

Imagine being free from hostility! Most of the time, Ping went from highly charged and ready to attack to calm as the glassy top of Lake Michigan on a still day. According to his coworkers, Ping had a history of bottling up emotions and exploding with rage at the oddest of times. He was reticent to communicate at other times. For Ping, anger would build and build until he couldn't hold it.

I was excited to hear Ping's insights about his relationship with hostility. I trusted his personal experience in his role as a Sales Director would show a clear contrast of how destructive anger can be and the significance of addressing this element of well-being.

The Interview

I had seen Ping months ago when we first started working with Easy Breezy, and the man who entered the room had changed, physically at least. When I first met Ping, his stance reminded me an animal crouched and ready to pounce. Now, he was dressed sharply, standing tall with a soft stride as he walked without pausing to sit for the interview.

Welcome, Ping. You are looking fine today. Have you been working out? What is different about you?

> I have. I work out most days and I feel great. Thanks for inviting me. I realized the first time we met I was not very pleasant with you. Which was weird because I felt I could benefit from spending some time with you. You are always welcoming. It's good to be here.

He adjusted the microphone on his lapel. Clearly, the filming thing was not new to him. We talked casually until I saw an opportunity to open the can of worms: his hostility.

Have you ever regretted how angry and volatile you were?

Yes, I always regretted the times I struck out with anger. I was full of shame and wanted to stop being so hurtful to people, but I had no idea where to begin. I was unaware that my behavior was a cycle. I used anger to manipulate people to do what I wanted. Honestly, deep down I was afraid, and anger gave me a way to protect myself from my fears and hurt.

I couldn't have told you that a few months ago as I had no idea of the harm I was inflicting. But now, it is fairly obvious. You probably want to know what I was afraid of, naturally, and I could give examples, but it was really fear in general. The heart of the matter is how I perceived the fear. For example, I was afraid I would fail my boss. If it appeared I might look bad to others in front of my boss, I often attacked someone else to move the attention away from me.

How did you attack them?

One time we were in a sales meeting, and I was asked to present how we failed to meet our sales numbers. The truth was we had missed by 25 percent, and I hadn't prepared our team to be ready for a new product that was projected to bring in the new sales. In the middle of my talk, our production manager, Reggie, said he had given me everything I needed to be successful. This interrupted how I wanted the presentation to be received, and rage shot through me. With fire in my eyes, I directed it at Reggie and started burning through him with questions.

"When exactly did you get me the materials, Reggie?" I asked him, knowing his answer would set him up for the next question. "And were those materials sent correctly?" I persisted, knowing multiple revisions happened, allowing me to create a case that we were not able to be ready until three weeks into the quarter.

Of course, that was a poor excuse as I had no real need for his materials, but he never interrupted my presentations again. And that was the point. I wanted people to know I was dangerous and not to be messed with. I needed them to fear me. Being unpredictable helped and was used as a weapon to control the story around the office. Intimidated people would never stab me in the back, not more than once anyway. And, most wouldn't dare attack me from the front. I was ruthless and quick with my tongue, a real dragon slayer.

Where did you learn to do this?

Ancient Chinese secret.

He began laughing and continued.

Remember the Calgon commercial from the 80s? It is true though. My mother is Chinese, and a sweetheart, until she is crossed. She taught me how to be vicious on the attack. Her enemies rarely saw it coming, and sometimes they were laughing as she stuck them with her dagger. Cunning, ruthless, and sweet. She loved to use her attack methods to control us as kids. I believe it is why I am so good, or was so good, at appearing calm as I raged and attacked without most knowing I was even angry. I had to veil it most of the time and resist my urge to attack shortly after working here. HR had been given my number, and I was warned not to use those strategies, as people had wised up. Then, I bottled things up, which led to even more destruction.

I was at a company picnic, doing the Ultimate Warrior team relay. In this event, once the winner succeeded in knocking the other off an inflatable platform, the next team member could begin their leg in the race. The loser, having been pushed off, had to get back up on the platform and touch a red circle in the middle before their team member could move on, thus giving a huge time advantage to the team of the winner.

So there we were, Caron and me. She looked all meek and sweet until you got to know her. She made some off-color remark about Asians not being athletic, "all brain and no brawn." Later, I discovered she was triggering memories of how my mother treated me, but in that moment, I just saw an opportunity to unleash on her. Instead of moving her aside and pushing her off, I played out a fantasy by lifting her high in the air and body slamming her to the mat. We had these foam cylinders and a body suit on for protection, but I felt joy seeing her face filled with horror as I slammed her down. That brought me such pleasure at the time.

I did it three times. She was horrified at how aggressive I was. After the third slam, she jumped off and said, "You win."

I raised my hands in victory but failed to notice the expression of disgust in the eyes of onlookers. A photo was shown to me later. In that moment, I looked like a monster.

I've been called a bully. People have interpreted my actions as sexist, racist, and hurtful. After that incident, and after seeing the photos and a video, I felt sadness. I looked pathetic and felt a lot of shame. It was uncomfortable to go to work every day feeling that. My anger masked the hurt of hidden wounds.

One day, I asked HR if I could get some help. They offered counseling and that was useful. I was able to see how my actions affected others, but the main wound was deep. Then I learned about the Optimal Being program and asked to sign up. The program helped unlock this hidden wound. I feel at peace now and have developed skills to address past issues that kept my anger alive and on a short fuse.

Ping, would you be comfortable sharing with us what this deeply hidden wound was?

> That's why I'm here. I came to share this with you. I would say the wound in me was not actually hidden to others. It was rather obvious to some. When I visited China years ago, a master healer mentioned it, but I was unwilling to hear. Essentially, it was a fear of failing and being exposed. My fear was hidden so deeply inside of me that I couldn't see it. I worked so hard to override my fear of failing by my being successful.

> But, this was covering up a deep feeling of never being enough. I lived with that feeling every day of my life. My family descended from peasants, and I wanted to be from prestige. But, I couldn't change my heritage. Deep down, I felt like a victim and as much as I tried to overcome the injustice in my mind, I resented my family heritage. I was angry and feared being inadequate forever and possibly passing it on to my next of kin. This was my deep hidden source of pain.

And?

> Through this awakened workforce project, I learned to look at my pain. I realized how good I am at my job. I noticed how happy I am with my family. I also recognized I live in a country that allows me the freedom to pursue all this. The only peasant left was the peasant in my mind, my false idea of who I was. I

changed how I saw my ancestors. Prior to this, I had kept them stuck as peasants in my mind.

My ancestors may have actually suffered greatly, but I was the one keeping the blame, hurt, and inadequacy alive. Once I admitted it was me who had kept the pain active, I was ready to open the door to healing, and I did.

I don't share this with many people, but as I let go judgments of my heritage, I saw many images of people I had never known flash across my mind's eye, and they were smiling. It was like I was seeing my ancestors and they were celebrating this too. That may sound strange, but I have heard others say similar things about generational wounds healing.

After that, I was more comfortable expressing myself and helping people see how hurt is kept alive in us.

What is life like now, as you are taking action to be free of hostility?

The blessings keep coming. One day, a new employee, Susan, did something in a meeting that would have triggered anger in me nine times out of nine. Well, she didn't think anything of it. She was challenging me, and I was aware the rest of the people in the room were anticipating a reaction from me. I noticed my anger didn't come up. It was like I was witnessing something profound. No anger, but I did notice people's response—

looking away, nervous twitches, shaking heads, and trying to get Susan's attention to warn her. I realized they had been responding to me that way for a long time, though I had never been aware of it.

It is certainly powerful when we can be a witness to the changes happening in real time. What happened next?

Well, I took a breath and interrupted the meeting. I let Susan know the reason the energy shifted in the room was because challenging me in the past had been a dangerous thing to do.

"I've not been very nice to people," I told her. "I felt completely inadequate at times, and when anything hinted other people might think me inadequate, I'd lash out at them until no one would challenge me. The truth is, I never really felt like I was enough until I started to embrace the wounds in me. I want you to know as a new employee here, Susan, that you can challenge me any time, and that goes for everybody. And if ever I react, I give you all permission to call me out. I mean it. Stand up, tell me what you see, and I promise to breathe, take responsibility for my actions, and wake up to what's really happening. If you do this, you will be doing me and everyone here a service. I wish I could be this aware all the time, but I don't know if that's possible yet. I apologize for interrupting the meeting, but I thought it was important that we start shifting together into a more constructive working relationship. Thanks for the opportunity to clear the air."

People were looking me in the eye, smiling, and saying thank you. There were some tears, and it opened up a brief conversation where people expressed the discomfort they'd felt when I reacted in anger. The tension was broken by laughter about the *miracle* that happened in conference room B. It was healing. Work has never been the same.

Ping smiled as he clearly was picturing the current work dynamic in his mind.

I used to hate coming to work. I didn't want to be here. I just wanted to hide. In fact, I would take as much sick time as I could without calling attention to it. I would just do whatever I could to get out of the office and away from people. I don't do that anymore. I wouldn't say I'm the most social person in the office, but I'm easy to get along with and having a bigger impact on the company.

Ping, it's fantastic. You sound like a new person. I don't recognize the guy I experienced in our first interactions. In conversing with you, you seem so relaxed and clear. I deeply appreciate what you've done, and this isn't easy work when you apply it to generational wounds like you've done. Sincerely, thank you for showing up. Anything else you would like to share about your changes?

One more thing. I've always known my areas of strength, but I would do my best to stretch out of that comfort zone and take on assignments I wasn't equipped to take on. I'd take them on because I thought I was supposed to. Now, I'm more honest with myself. Instead of putting myself in a situation where I am going to let the company down, I communicate with my team and say, "Hey, I'm really skilled at certain things and not others," so I am able to assign projects to the folks who will do them the best and with the greatest ease. Or, I ask for permission to learn alongside someone and become stronger in certain areas of interest. I'm more honest with myself and the organization, and everyone benefits.

My stress is lower, I'm having more fun, and I'm encouraging people. Now that I'm okay with who I am in so many other areas, I recognize how valuable other people are and work to honor who they are as people. It's been pretty cool for me and them.

Thank you, Ping. I heard you say anger informs you that something's off inside yourself, that some expectation you hold isn't being met, and when you are willing to look at it and face whatever it is honestly, you have an opportunity to choose consciously. When you resist it and miss the message you are giving yourself through anger, you are missing an opportunity to have an optimal outcome. Is that a fair summary?

Yes, and the way I heard it said best is that a person's IQ goes to zero when they are acting from anger and hostility. And, the outcome will always be destructive. It was easy for me to go to my drug of choice, anger, but it was ineffective.

Thank you so much, Ping!

Interview Notes

I sat and closed my eyes for a few moments and relaxed into my breath after Ping left. Since anger is something I struggled with, that was a challenging interview for me. He had some great insights, though, that served as a reminder to me to continue the practices in the Optimal Being program.

Ping has transformed not only his personal life, but the working life of his team with direct, open communication. His current ability to take responsibility for his feelings, past and present, is truly exceptional.

The Well-Being Element of Anger Resolved

We do not need to explain how hostility and angry outbursts damage an organization. There is a reason that HR departments often use the phrase *hostile work environment* to describe situations of distress and unethical behaviors in the workplace. These situations reduce productivity and contribute to high employee turnover, both detrimental to a company's profits and eventual survivability.

You may not have a relationship with anger, or you may have it as a good friend you call on regularly. You may judge it or you may celebrate it. You are unique in how anger shows up specifically for you and in how it is triggered by your experiences. The good news is that you can be more conscious in your anger. You can become aware of its effects on others. You can notice it early and use the Optimal Being tools to address the underlying cause before it gets out of hand. Resolving anger saves time, eases relationships, and reduces regrets. Productivity amplifies as teams work in harmony more consistently. Shifting this element in your organization has so many benefits. See more about how it plays out personally and organizationally as a challenge or when optimal by scanning this QR code with your phone's camera.

QR code URL: optimalbeing.live/well-being-info-graphic

Chapter 8

Terina: Understanding and Accepting Universal Laws of Living

Terina is Greek, meaning to *reap* or *harvest*.

Terina's chosen name is so fitting when considering our next element of well-being: Universal Laws that govern our lives. Terina published a book this year about her walk with addiction. I wanted to show Terina I was familiar with her work, so I placed a copy of her book on the table where I'd be interviewing her. I noted it is quite popular among counselors who want to share hope for recovery with their clients. It surprised me to see her name on the interview list. Honestly, I wasn't expecting her to join me as I had heard she was *too cool* for what we were doing.

Terina had been ignorant of the Universal Laws of living and had experienced the consequences. Having read her story in the pages of her book, I paused in appreciation for how far Terina had traveled in her journey, and I felt my heart open at the prospect of learning from her myself.

The Interview

Terina entered with the confidence of someone who knew herself well. Her long white dress had a black sash held in place by a silver-ringed loop. A tattoo of the immaculate heart emblazoned her right arm. She asked which chair was hers and proceeded toward it, standing politely until I was ready to sit.

Thanks for coming, Terina. Are you ready for this?

> As ready as I'll ever be. You have quite the setup. I was thinking it would be more casual, but you have lights, cameras . . . looks like all that is needed is a little action.

She laughed at her double entendre humor.

> But seriously, can you cut out anything too personal, as I am sensitive about revealing too much?

Again, she was playfully kidding as she held her tell-all memoir to her face with a big grin.

I can tell we are going to have a good time, Terina. Let's get rolling. Would you begin by sharing why you are doing this interview?

Well, you know about the law of reciprocity, right? The world gave me an opportunity to overcome one of the greatest challenges a person could go through, and now that I am on the other side of it, I believe I have a responsibility to share it. It may appear we live on the shoulders of giants, but within these giants are many thousands of people who discovered something and chose to share. Most never saw themselves as giants, and yet their Herculean efforts affected the courses of lives: friends, neighbors, communities, congregations— actually the whole planet. Human beings are inspired to share what we learn. We are inspired to grow and evolve as a species—together.

Sharing allows us to let go of *our baby* for the benefit of others and then move on to what is next in life. As we give, we receive. Give a smile and it will come back. Your smiling might remind another person to smile, and ten people see that person and smile, and it goes on and on and on.

A real example: Our Art Director saw a woman entering an apartment building and had a moment he described as surreal. He says he saw a flash of light in the woman's eyes, and he smiled in awe. He went home that night and nicked the garage door with his car. Suddenly, struck with disappointment, he entered the house and told his wife. She smiled, and he saw this spark again, but this time in his wife's eyes. He was overcome with peace.

The garage door repair company showed up the next week as he was heading out to his car. A woman—the woman he saw at the apartment—got out of the repair truck, made eye contact, and began crying. She said she needed to leave and got back into her truck. He ran to her truck door to ask what happened.

She replied, "I was on my way to visit my dying grandfather when I noticed you smile at me. I went inside, and he had passed. I kept thinking of your smile. I was heading to see him as he was *on his way out*. I had asked him one night before he passed to give me a sign that he was okay on the other side. I believe you were that sign. But, I've been doubting it, so I prayed for confirmation that it was truly the sign I asked for. Now, out of all the people who live in this huge city, I show up at *your* house. I got my confirmation."

You see, I often have experiences I can't explain. We don't really know what a thing is or what it is for, but I knew it was important to be here today, Ethan, just as our Art Director knew to smile at that woman and nick the garage door.

She shared her story with authenticity, and I was enthralled.

What was life like before you learned about Universe Laws and began consciously honoring them?

Okay. This is a doozy. First, I had perceived myself as a victim most of my life, and I believed someone was going to get hurt and, most likely, it was going to be me. I was always trying to help, save, and protect other people. It was important for me to find people who shared the philosophy: *We are in this together.* But I believed the *this* we were all in was ugly, twisted, and full of sharp objects that injure when bumped.

My parents died when I was a kid, and I grew up in my aunt and uncle's basement. My uncle had a friend who used to come over to drink. One night, the friend came downstairs. No one ever came down at night. There was nothing down there but the furnace and me. He didn't want the furnace. Needless to say, it didn't go well for me that night.

She paused, took a breath, and then another as she shook her head. I waited, allowing her to take her time and to share only what she wanted to share.

I was fifteen. I know many who have had similar experiences. Did you know one out of every six women in the United States has been the victim of sexual assault?

I nodded.

I tried to escape, but I couldn't.

She paused again.

Sometime later, he passed out on my bed. I grabbed a T-shirt and shorts and made my way upstairs where my uncle was doing dishes. I was crying, shaking all over, and scared. He put two and two together and told me to call the police. I pulled myself together and called.

Meanwhile, I heard my uncle running up to his room and back down the stairs. Then, I heard a gunshot. I don't know that I had ever heard a gun go off, but I knew what it was and what it meant. That sound reverberated through every nerve of my body as I hung up the phone.

Of course, the dispatcher on the line did know what a gunshot sounded like.

My uncle came upstairs crying and held my hand, "Ain't no one ever going to touch you like that again."

I was in complete shock at this point, unable to think or feel or make a single decision. I followed him out to the front porch where, minutes later, an ambulance, fire engine, and three police squad cars raced up our street with sirens blaring. Guns drawn, they pointed to us to come off the porch and lie on the ground. Our hands were cuffed, and we were held at gunpoint until they wheeled my assailant from the house, alive and in a lot of pain. I was also in a lot of pain, but I was in handcuffs with a gun pointed at me. I never felt more betrayed than I did at that moment.

I see now that my perpetrator looked like a victim, and my savior looked like the perpetrator to the police. While my uncle's friend was rushed to the hospital, we were questioned. I could barely string a sentence together as I stood shivering on the lawn. I wanted to take a shower. I wanted to escape, to be anywhere else. I certainly was going into physical shock. I was finally taken to the hospital for tests to verify my story, and my uncle was arrested.

What a mess my aunt came home to. Her husband was in jail for attempted murder, her niece had been raped, and her house was on the news for all of New York to see. Everything in our world was different, as if life had exploded all over itself.

You want to know what was really fu**ed up? I wanted him to live. If he died, I was afraid I'd never see my uncle again. But, I was just as scared that if he lived, he might do more harm to me. I rode an emotional tidal wave as I thought of the attack and what might lie ahead. Every option I considered brought a fresh onslaught of pain as my thoughts became a vicious tornado, swirling in circles that kept growing wider and wider. The doctor gave me some medication, and I cried myself to sleep.

I now know sleep is the best thing for someone who has been assaulted. It allows for mental healing as the brain sorts stuff out. It also stops the very thing I was doing: reliving and reinforcing the trauma. My last thought before sleep was that I was somehow lucky. My folks had died early in my life, but I had people who were willing to sacrifice everything for me. I felt grateful.

Unfortunately, that was not the end of the pain. I lived on in fear. I perceived threats everywhere. Yet, I took crazy risks, in spite of my experience. Twice, once in high school and once in college, I was nearly raped. I found myself in situations that were unsafe, usually involving alcohol. Once, I was at a diner in a sketchy neighborhood at 3:00 a.m. after a night of drinking and encountered some guy in the ladies' bathroom. . .

Terina looked up, saw me crying, and asked what was happening.

I am feeling some intense emotion surfacing as I listen to you share such horrible experiences. I suppose I felt joy at your uncle's desire to avenge you. He "took care of business," so to speak. He must have felt like he failed to protect you and was trying to make up for that failure in some small way. He was protecting other potential victims from a monster.

I could tell she did not agree with me as she shook her head.

> I know it sounds like the right thing was for my uncle to avenge me, but it was not like you picture in your imagination. No one heralded my uncle as a hero, and he certainly was messed up for quite some time. He reacted without thinking. He had it in his head that I was his responsibility, and he couldn't handle the idea of failing my parents. He snapped. And, he never looked at me the same again. I was a reminder of his failure. There were many times I think he blamed me for what happened.
>
> I was terrified of the basement. I tried living upstairs after that, but my aunt wanted me to cover every inch of my skin all the time. I had been so comfortable in my skin before, moving about with or without clothes as I felt like it. I grew afraid to even step out of the bathroom after my shower without being fully clothed.
>
> Now, I see that I was a living, breathing, walking reminder of a trauma they neither wanted nor knew how to process. In fact, none of us processed our emotions. So, I felt like it was all on me: the pain and the responsibility. I came to see myself as a *victim* in every waking moment.

Finally, my aunt suggested it would be better for everyone if I went back to sleeping in the basement. I did. Of course, I started having nightmares and would wake up in a sweat. Next came the panic attacks. I soon discovered drugs prevented the attacks and the nightmares. I began using infrequently, but by the end of my sophomore year, I had become a regular customer of the local dealer, nicknamed The Garden Store. I had found something to *rescue* me from my pain.

Soon, I was buying direct and even selling and distributing whenever I had a chance. I was not at home much, often finding reasons to party. It could have cost me the opportunity to go to college, but thankfully, I was born with a great memory and made it through high school.

Terina paused and whispered under her breath,

Bastard.

There was some sadness in her expression, and she took a deep breath and kissed a cross that hung around her neck.

Bless you, Bernard.

Has he passed? I assume Bernard is the "bastard"?

No, he's still alive. I see now that I still judge him, and I was offering a blessing for him to be at peace about it. I've done so with everyone in my life. The pain of holding onto judgment and anger is too great to bear, and I hope he has made peace with what he did.

How are you so compassionate toward this guy?

He's not my enemy. I see what you mean, though. The pain of revenge is far greater than the peace that comes with true forgiveness. It took me a while to learn that, but it is always true.

I didn't know it at the time, but one day I was inspired intuitively that my mother had been raped by a friend of my father's. My aunt later confirmed it. I was actually conceived when my mother was being raped. As strange as it sounds, it was like I could remember the thoughts and feelings of hate, hurt, and betrayal.

My mother and father's pain, even though they are gone, seemed to be alive in me in some way, and I was either going to resent them for it or allow it to heal in me. I've spent the last decade seeking a way to heal. It was like I had an internal radio broadcasting station blasting out in high volume: *come abuse me.* Desiring to dispel of this broadcast and the victim mentality, I chose to change.

Now, I am able to stay present in almost all situations regarding any kind of abuse, while viewing others with love and compassion. That is how I discovered my attackers had light in them just like the rest of us.

I understand how it must have happened, that they were abused in some way and they took their pain and abused others with it. It doesn't excuse or condone their behavior. Still, it does show us that we have an opportunity to heal cycles of abuse.

These cycles can show up at work too. In my department, we lost a client whose trust was betrayed by a member of our team. People stealing ideas or talking ill of a friend or embezzling are all forms of this betrayal of trust and the energy of violation. It can be changed. I've seen it firsthand, and it is powerful. These patterns can change.

Changing these unhealthy dynamics and patterns is truly one of the core benefits of learning and practicing the tools of the Optimal Being program. I'm thrilled about the levels of healing in your life and all your work to change old patterns. Would you tell us more about how you see the world now?

It is so much easier for me to see how the world reflects our thoughts, feelings, and beliefs. It shows up in individuals, races, creeds, companies, nations, and so on. We need to realize the only way something can show up *outside ourselves* is if it exists within us.

I am learning to create consciously as the loving human I am. Anything else is going to feed the victim/persecutor/savior triangle, which is pervasive around our world right now. I believe we can change this ongoing pattern on all levels, from micro to macro.

Imagine the greatest emotional traumas and pains, such as discrimination, abuse, addictions, poverty, and so many crimes being healed in our society through people willing to embrace their hidden realities and corresponding pain with love, allowing inspiration to create lasting change.

If it can happen in me, it's possible in all of us.

My eyes and heart have opened to see a perfect and Lawful order in my life. I was carrying unhealed energy of sexual abuse and attracted it in the form of people who perpetrated their own unhealed trauma and abuse memories. Because they did not discover methods to heal, they did whatever they could to alleviate the symptoms of their pain, essentially, by abusing others. We attract experiences based on the frequencies inside us. You know, our thoughts, feelings, emotions, and beliefs. The unhealed matching frequencies inside me drew these experiences to me.

Would you say a few words about what you mean by matching frequency?

As you know, we have a law of resonance in the world. A C note in music can be heard by tapping a C tuning fork. Put this vibrating tuning fork next to a second

C fork, and the second will begin vibrating too. The frequencies match. Put the vibrating C tuning fork next to a B tuning fork, and nothing will happen to the B. The frequencies don't match.

I carried, subconsciously of course, the frequencies of betrayal and fear, so I attracted people who matched. It is automatic. Just like the second C tuning fork resonated with the first C. When a person's anger is up, anyone in proximity with a matching frequency will feel it. If that person has a pattern of running when someone is expressing anger, they will begin feeling like they need to leave the room. If they don't feel they can leave, they may begin feeling anxiety about what possibly could unfold.

Ever notice the mood shift in a meeting? That's an example of resonance playing out in a group. Personally, I know I need to accept whatever surfaces in me and take the opportunity to invite love to heal any fear or hostility I am experiencing. Then I have the opportunity to be restored fully by aligning with the frequency of love.

I can embrace certain things on my own, but healing happens much quicker when we do it together. Imagine this same meeting. What if everyone stopped when the mood shifted, took deep breaths, and addressed what was surfacing in themselves. Then, when the group remembered their true nature—love—they would allow fear and hostility to dissolve. Peace, openness, and healing would take place. Imagine the creativity and solutions that could arise in that moment!

That is why so much is changing in our company. We are all committed to this. We want this for ourselves and each other. It is fun and much better than the often-dysfunctional approaches we mastered as habits before.

What is an example of an approach you used?

Instead of healing, I suppressed everything with drugs. It was like having a rabid dog in a cage in my living room and covering it with a blanket so I couldn't see it.

The good news is I don't do that any longer. I am off the drugs. I faced the truth. I am free. I talk about it from wisdom instead of pain, and this has helped many people, especially women, find peace. Interestingly enough, what I use to heal is taught in a number of places, including as an area of focus in the Optimal Being program. It was timed perfectly to help me let go of the victim mentality I still carried.

As we wrap up, what would you say to people who might be nervous about revealing such intimate details of their past?

To be clear, no one has to share details like this. Complete privacy is allowed; I just find it benefits me to share. I've seen the beneficial impact on others when they hear my story. It is up to each person though. In fact, you don't even need to be in a group. People can do Optimal Being entirely on their own if they prefer privacy and have the discipline to do so.

Excellent clarification. Thank you. What would say in closing about these Universal Laws?

If you knew about the law of gravity and were in your right mind, would you jump from a ten-story building without a parachute or another way to work with the forces of wind and gravity? Living out of alignment with Law is like jumping and then blaming something external for the result your experience—like the air for not slowing you down or God for not changing gravity to save you or a loved one for not catching you.

Gravity won't assess whether to pull you to the street below. It just pulls whether you are male, female, brown, white, old, or young. Gravity pulls. Universal Laws, like the law of gravity, affect everyone. The Law of resonance. The Law of giving and receiving and all the rest. Taking time to learn, understand, and honor these Laws is essential to living a wonderful life.

Anything else you would like to share?

Just that I see how this program is transforming our whole team, and I know our leadership group has been doing it as well. There's a confidence, trust, and rhythm to things that feel so good.

Terina, thank you so much for being here. You are a real-life superhero, moving through your experiences and now sharing your story with others.

I am thankful too. Truly.

Interview Notes

Terina reminded me that life is not all roses after adopting the principles of the Optimal Being program, but participants learn to embrace life with all its ebbs and flows. Over time, like with her experiences with sexual assault, we learn to embrace the positive and the negative events in our lives in order to propel forward. If we believe the Laws are *in our way* or *against us* as Terina thought, we can frame ourselves or others as *victims*, preventing an opportunity to fully live using these forces of nature.

Since we are always creating—either aligned with our Optimal Being or not—being in this high vibrational state is a priority for Terina and for me as well.

The Well-Being Element of Understanding and Acceptance of Universal Laws

Opening the door to creating a life in alignment with the Laws of the Universe is extraordinary and supports an optimal life. These Laws affect everyone and can be understood, embraced, and honored. Ignorance of them does not negate their effect on us. They exist. They govern. The way to a life of happiness and well-being is dependent on aligning with Law.

There are Laws that govern the operation of the human mind, body, emotions, relationships, finances, spirituality, and more. Some people are unaware of these Laws of Living, and ignorance is definitely not bliss. Martin Luther King Jr. stated it so clearly as he addressed why people suffer. He said, "There are moral laws of the universe just as abiding as the physical laws, and when we disobey [violate] these moral laws we suffer tragic consequences."[13]

Laws are understood through experience. For example, if you are living as taught in the Optimal Being program, you will experience inner alignment and joy. The world will start changing to correspond with your inner changes. This is an example of a law. Your outer world will reflect your inner world. Angry inside? You will find the outer world providing ample opportunity for you to feel your anger. Are you internally happy and joyful? The world will reflect that too.

Based on your thoughts, feelings, beliefs, words, and your focus, you utilize the **Law of Resonance** through vibrations and frequencies. These vibrations will always match what you think, feel, and believe. Your speech will then match these vibrations. People aligned as an Optimal Being speak, resonate, and create in alignment.

When your words and your intentions are congruent with your true beliefs and feelings, they will be mirrored back to you through your relationships and experiences. The resonance you project into the world establishes a **rhythm** in your life. When you are in alignment with your Optimal Being, you resonate higher frequency thoughts and words and thus attract experiences into your life more quickly. If you have resistance and an absence of alignment, you generate lower frequencies, substantially slowing down your outcomes. This is why one person may take three days to accomplish something, while another takes weeks or months to do something similar. It is not good or bad, just as gravity is not good or bad. It just is. When we know this, we can address it consciously and utilize another law, the **Law of Attraction**, to clarify and align with the manifestation of our desires.

Realistically, most people unconsciously perceive themselves as victims in the world and do not realize their role in the outcomes of their life. Those who *do* have an awareness of their responsibility to function in alignment dramatically accelerate desired optimal outcomes in their lives. Essentially, when you connect to your inner guidance system, it leads to living as an Optimal Being. Your thoughts, feelings, words, and beliefs will be in alignment and consistently produce optimal outcomes with greater ease and efficiency.

Shifting this element in your organization has so many benefits. See more about how it plays out personally and organizationally as a challenge or when optimal by scanning this QR code with your phone's camera.

QR code URL: optimalbeing.live/well-being-info-graphic

Chapter 9

Ozzie: Health and Vitality

Ozzie, in Hebrew, simply means *strong*.

Ozzie is a forty-something computer programmer at Easy Breezy who has experienced ups and downs with his health. He trained to run a marathon once, but never quite made it. Ozzie twisted his ankle stepping off the Dumbo ride at Disney the day before the race. He was so discouraged, he skipped the marathon and hobbled through Animal Kingdom instead.

After that, he abandoned his eating, exercising, and healthy habits. He gained fifteen pounds in three months and, for the next few years, rode the highs and lows between inspired to get healthy and feeling it was not worth the trouble. Ozzie's number-one well-being challenge was the element of being open to the truth and any stress that can come with it. A close second, though, was this element of nutrition and physical health. Both were in *crisis*, or major challenges. Though he completed the base Optimal Being program several months before this interview, it wasn't until three months ago that he began to make consistent progress in these areas.

Throughout Ozzie's experience with Optimal Being, I always found him a dapper dresser. Today was no exception. While programmers may sport a typical look, Ozzie was consistently eccentric and colorful. He walked in sporting a long-sleeved red silk shirt under a blue sparkling vest, and a pair of the coolest blue jeans I had ever seen: Brayen Rock Revival's shredded with parts of the American flag showing through the holes.

The Interview

Ozzie came in laughing and gave me a fist bump as he glided toward his chair.

Ozzie, you look happy to be here.

He took his ear buds out, still smiling.

What's that? I was listening to some old stand-up.

I was saying you look happy to be here, but now I understand. It's good to see you. You look good. What is happening with your health?

> Oh, you don't mess around. Just get right down to it. Well, if you must know, I am not happy with where things are at the moment. I indulged in a latte, full fat, this morning, and I am tempted by the most amazing looking glazed donut sitting right outside that door. Are you trying to mess me up?

His smile and joking tone brought a smile to my face as well.

No, I was not aware of the donuts. They weren't there when I arrived. I suppose you can go get one if you like. I mean, I am not one to turn down a donut.

> I didn't say *donuts*. One. One glazed donut. It was in Jada's hands, and I almost grabbed it, but she looked so determined to keep it. Oh well.

> So, you want to know about my health? I'm doing much, much, better. I used to think I was healthy because I ran, but I realized I was only running to prove I could. Someone told me running was impossible for me, you see. It really had little to do with health. My gym teacher teased me when I was in high school, telling me I ran like a girl, which was insulting . . . to the girls.

He was very amused at his delivery, as was I.

Anyway, one day I told him I would run a marathon, and he would have to eat shit and die on that day . . .

He's still alive. In fact, I was at Animal Kingdom on the Safari ride aptly named *Kill-a-man-jaro* on the day I was supposed to run the marathon. An elephant was doing his business when I remembered my words to my gym teacher. Right then and there I looked him up on social media and saw a picture of him with his grandkids. He was still very much alive. Wasn't any way I was going to kill him after seeing those cute grandkids. So, I gave up running.

Apparently, that was the only reason I was exercising: *revenge*. You know what sucks about revenge? Not having it anymore. I was empty and filled the emptiness with—you saw this coming—donuts, plus Big Macs, and ice cream. I poured myself into work and watched my body mutate. It was a sad process, but one I needed in order to see how *off* I was. I was not sure whether it would change, but something came up in the MindShifter tool I used in Optimal Being.

I remembered I never really liked myself. Back in high school, I questioned why I was even alive and what the point of life was. I thought about taking my life. It came flooding back, and I asked my Program Guide for some help. Apparently, this was beyond her abilities, so she turned me on to one of the Optimal Being Mentors. That was magical. I mean, really magical.

Is there anything you want to share about that call?

Well, let's just say I was willing to open up a wound that had haunted me since I was a young kid. I wouldn't say the Mentor even did that much as far as I could tell. But, he had a way of asking questions that allowed me to see the truth, and he supported me as I faced it, reminding me to breathe and encouraging me to feel the pain surfacing with the memories. I was face-to-face in my spirit with my four-year-old self, and I asked him what he wanted most, and he answered: *love*.

The process continued, and I asked that *four-year-old* if he could tell me, or show me, what *love* was to him. He hugged me in my mind's eye and told me I was the one who needed to answer that question. He touched my heart with his hand, and I saw the answer. It was like a movie where the picture suddenly comes into focus, you know? And I felt this presence, like *more than me* was there. Now I understand that love was there. Though it took a bit of time to fully embrace, I knew I had made *everything* a priority over this love. I had been so focused on being what I thought I needed to be in order to get love, that I missed the obvious.

I was unable to see what was inside me because I was so focused on the outer picture of what I perceived was expected. That day, I made a commitment to myself to do whatever was necessary to heal any childhood wounds and embrace truth. I went for a juicy cheeseburger and fries to celebrate. I hadn't learned that part yet.

What part is that?

Well, I used to reward myself with food. If I believed I did something worth praise, I would get a treat, in this case a cheeseburger and fries. That was a common go-to. It was a memory of my childhood. We didn't have much, so it was unusual for us to go out for *treats*. We were shocked if Mom or Dad would take us for a donut, or McDonald's, Dairy Queen, or anything we thought was *good*.

I loved when we would have company over, because I knew the bowl of M&Ms and other treats would be out. I scarfed them down as quickly as I could, often ending the evening overstuffed and with a headache from eating so many sweets. I believed other people were more important than me because those snacks were not in the house unless there was a party. I put a high value on this type of snack and often ate it as an adult because I wanted to feel valued, loved. Twisted? Yes.

But, how do you untwist something like that? I will tell you how I did it.

Yes, please. Others will have their own stories about these types of foods, so sharing how you transformed will certainly be appreciated.

He adjusted himself in his chair to lean forward as if to share a secret with a friend.

> Okay, there were three major steps I took, all of which I learned in the Optimal Tools, which was key to this whole change. The first major step was getting out of my head. I had all these ideas and rules in my head associated with health, nutrition, being fit, and the like.

Such as?

> Okay, well, I hated working out as it reminded me of the jocks in high school that I judged as better than me. I hated eating well 'cause it reminded me of my mother telling me to eat well.

> All I wanted was a house that had *good* food to eat, which to me meant cookies, Doritos, Cheetos, and other things I was missing out on because we were *apparently too poor*. If we had money, we could afford all that *good* food. I associated money with junk food. When I started working and making money, you can guess what I did. I bought whatever junk food I wanted. I told myself I was worth it. The problem was, it was not real food, and a body can't process endless supplies of junk food. These were the ideas I had though. I had

to get out of my head where all those ideas lived and ask for help. I sought out health experts to understand how to eat. I shifted to more organic and pesticide-free foods. There's some junk food in the house, but I don't eat it often. Funny enough, it is mostly there for parties. Hmm . . . maybe Mom was not buying healthy foods due to lack of money after all. Maybe she cared about our health and wanted us to eat fruits and vegetables because our bodies needed those things.

The second major step was to let go of what I thought I knew, like *Mom didn't buy any good food* and *Mom cared more for guests than her own family* and all the rest of the beliefs I held. As I learned what gave my body energy, I had to face more and more of my beliefs and challenge my patterns.

The third major step was to allow my body to interrupt my habits. I literally had a conversation with my body and said, "I don't know what is best right now regarding food. I am willing to learn. Interrupt me when I am out of alignment and I allow me to eat what is healthy for my body."

You are serious? You said that to your body?

Damn straight. I was serious about being healthy.

So, how did your body respond?

It wasn't how my body responded, but how I listened. My body was always ready and willing to support me in eating the best—or optimal—foods for me. I wasn't always willing to act on the information, but interruptions sure came. For months, I was working at home and would have this urge to go to the pantry and get chips, crackers, and other snacks.

The resistance grew in me, though, and I found myself one day just standing in the pantry. I felt overwhelmed about a work-related project and I noticed my feelings. But, instead of eating, I stood breathing and feeling the overwhelming sensations. After a few minutes, I walked out and found myself back at my desk, never having eaten anything. It was that day I realized I had those resistant urges before but overrode them.

I started to notice my body-mind system serving me better. I realized when I felt overwhelmed, I ate. I asked if there was anything to learn, and I heard an inner voice answer, "It is okay to eat snacks, but only do so when guided to. Feel your feelings and allow the patterns to change." As hard as it may be to believe this was true, it was what I needed to hear in order to begin actually changing my habits.

Soon, I would see images in my mind of carrots and celery with natural peanut butter sometimes and pretzels, another. Slowly, my desire for nourishing foods grew, and I shifted away from unhealthy options and started eating only what I was inspired to eat. I began to trust my choices, and I found myself learning in the process. One day, I was even inspired to go running again. It felt so natural. I noticed other exercises were inspired too. I began Rollerblading, playing tennis, enjoying work around the house, and slowly, my body changed shape.

And how have things changed at work for you?

I'm feeling like a rock star—happy, loose, engaged, productive, and having fun. I really am, and I can honestly tell you that, because I was not always that way. I am energized, I love my job, I feel good, and I am a big reason we are doing the Optimal Being program as part of this awakened workforce project. After a board presentation from Randy, our CHRO, regarding the well-being crisis at Easy Breezy, Yori, our CEO, sought me out. He shared some of the data Randy discovered and said the board was committed to doing this right. Seeing a leader like that be vulnerable was new to me, but he genuinely wanted this. He was trying to improve himself, too, and as he'll share with you, also follow through on an inspiration from his youth. Though I was still new to using the tools, the changes in me had been noticeable. Of course, I am one part of a much bigger thing taking place and appreciate the role I played. This has become a great place to work.

He raised his hands in the air and stomped his feet up and down as he danced in his chair.

I love this place. I love my life!

Interview Notes

You can see how making this element a priority has changed things for Ozzie. He's not the only one. There are now healthy snack options around the office, and an upgraded food service allows for people to easily choose options supporting their alertness and well-being throughout the day. The exercise facility on campus is amazing and well used too. No one was more impacted, perhaps, than Yori, whose interview is next.

The Well-Being Element of Health and Vitality

In recent years, companies have begun addressing this element of well-being in their workforces. From exercise facilities onsite to fitness challenges to healthier food options, business leaders have come to realize that a healthy workforce is a productive workforce.

Ergonomic considerations, such as standing desks, supportive wrist pads, and custom-made chairs, have lowered the cost of healthcare and reduced sick days away from work. Fitness trackers are distributed at no cost. But what if these pro-health practices are the tip of the iceberg?

All the elements of well-being are tightly woven with each other. Imagine what can be gained in physical vitality when the entire person is moved to wholeness, wellness, and presence in regard to their well-being.

Can you imagine this for your workforce? For yourself?

Shifting this element in your organization has so many benefits. See more about how it plays out personally and organizationally as a challenge or when optimal by scanning this QR code with your phone's camera.

QR code URL: optimalbeing.live/well-being-info-graphic

Chapter 10

Yori: Use of Will

Yori is Japanese for *trustworthy* or *reliable*.

Yori is the head of the organization and, along with Ozzie, is the reason this awakened workforce project was adopted at Easy Breezy. Have you ever seen someone who was humble and yet was mysteriously remarkable all at once? His chosen name, *Yori*, doesn't even begin to describe his commitment to this company and its workforce.

Yori was born in France and lived through a tumultuous upbringing before moving to the United States back in the 1970s. His mother was his hero growing up, as she kept him and his brother safe from a landlord who was feared to have been responsible for a number of deaths in their community. His mother would walk him and his brother home after school and never let them be alone for the *ghetto killer* to snatch.

One day, a man who had never been in their neighborhood asked Yori's mother for directions to find the landlord. She told the man to be wary. She gave him a small knife and said, "Hide this and bring it to me after you have your meeting. It will serve you to keep it in your back-left pocket. I will be with you in spirit while you are visiting. Return the knife to me after. Now, go."

Young Yori was sitting nearby, overheard the conversation, and discreetly followed the man. Yori peeked through a window to the landlord's office and saw the landlord pull a gun on the man. The landlord forced the visitor to put his hands behind his back and his goon tied the man's hands with a rope. They left him tied up and sitting in the chair. Yori watched him reach into his left pocket and pull out the knife from Yori's mother. The visitor was free within moments and made his way safely back.

The man returned the knife, and two days later, three airplane tickets and 10,000 francs arrived by courier. Yori, his brother, and mother packed and left for Chicago.

Yori always wanted to return this favor and assist others. The awakened workforce project is a direct result of the man who saved his family. He calls that man Alexander.

Yori had a 1980s *Miami Vice* look to him as he walked in with white pants, tan sport coat, and light blue T-shirt. He was wearing red Converse shoes, and his moustache was tight to his lip. I had seen Yori before and almost laughed at his outfit. It was unexpected.

The Interview

Welcome, Yori!

> It's a costume. I can go and change if it's distracting. We are making a point to our marketing team to *Come Out of the 80s* with our ad budget. It worked. We try to have fun around here.

Nice, and no need. Your look works for me. I like a leader who is willing to do this type of thing. First off, can you let me know why you call the man who paid your way to America Alexander? Was that his name?

> No one has ever asked me that before. A teacher told me Alexander the Great was a man she admired, and I found out that Alexander meant *protector of man*, and since I didn't know the man's actual name . . . I went with Alexander. He, in a way, is why we are here today. He greatly inspired my life.

Well, whoever and wherever you are, Alexander, we all thank you. Your element of well-being, Yori, is an interesting one. Fulfilling goals and commitments is one I would expect to be a strength of yours, but it was the biggest opportunity for you to improve. Tell me more.

At first, I resisted believing I had an issue in this element, but I found I had been leaving a number of things to chance. My mother was something of a mystic. The knife given to the man who is responsible for our move to this beautiful country is an example. My mother was very specific about where to put it and what it was to be used for. I asked her how she knew on the plane leaving France. You know what she said to me?

"I did not know anything. I only listened to God."

Infuriating. She listened to *God*. I wanted to know how she did it so I could learn to be as awesome as this hero mom of mine. Unfortunately, I was not hearing God speak to me. I didn't even listen to my mother half the time. Oh well. She will be remembered as a saint for all the good she did in this world. She is the other reason I wanted every employee to have access to this program.

She taught me that we all have a way to hear God's voice and that it will come in the form we are most open to hearing it. Some, she said, can hear it in people; others, in animals or places; and some have such a clearly tuned speaker system that they hear directly. She heard directly.

I love how your company teaches people to tune in to their intuitive guidance system, which I now know is an option for everyone. I can attest to how it is reshaping our organization. The incredible, positive changes keep coming!

The program is simple enough, and universal to people of any faith or no faith. Plus, we like its pragmatic approach. I would not say I am listening to God like my mother, but I am inspired by something; a deeper knowing and confidence. That *something* is always for the benefit of myself and our teams. So, when I was called out for not following through on my commitments, I felt irritated, perhaps jealous, like I was when my mom was hearing God's voice. I wanted to follow through and was willing to learn.

Can you share how it is different? How you know it is different?

You bet. It starts with my purpose. I was building a business to make money so I could use the profits to help people. Turns out, I was mistaken. When I did the *primary and secondary purpose exercise* with my Optimal Being Mentor, I discovered I was *Doing* things in order to *Have* what I thought I needed so I could someday *Be* how I wanted to be.

Now, this wasn't the first time I had heard this, as it is a common Buddhist teaching, but it was the first time I really understood what it meant. Rex, my Mentor, challenged me to *Be* first, so my *Doing* would flow from my *Being*. Then I was to trust I would set ideal goals and the follow-through would come. So I learned to meditate before creating any plans, and all my goals supported one of the plans. All the plans supported my purposes. If a goal did not line up with a plan, I said no and moved on. Quickly all my goals were lining up to be easier to follow through on. This early change for me, learning to properly use my will, was a game changer.

One of our plans is to have a culture that attracts and supports the very best of humanity showing up daily at Easy Breezy. I started asking what we wanted to *Be* in our culture. We want harmony, collaboration, support, high impact, low drama, and great results. A team manages goals daily in support of our optimal culture plan, and it is unfolding faster than I anticipated.

As CEO, though, don't you do things CEOs must do, including those you may not want to do?

Are you a parent? Are there parenting tasks you don't particularly want to do?

Yes. I am. Father of three. Oh, I get it. I chose to be a parent, and I am responsible for certain actions as a parent, so I don't choose whether I like changing diapers—it's part of being a parent.

Almost. Now, shift your mindset from you *have to* change diapers to you *get to* change diapers as a parent. It is one of the joys of parenthood. This little life you love immensely would have a diaper rash if you were to leave the child in the dirty diaper. You, in the presence of love that you are, will enjoy changing the diaper to support your child having healthy skin and to be comfortable. No one wants a messy diaper, and you are the light in their life with a solution. Now you can choose to resent the task because it is your turn or enjoy being with and caring for your child.

That is how I view some of the activities I *have* to do. I do them with joy because my purpose is bigger than the activity. My purpose requires action in order to be fulfilled. I can do it begrudgingly or happily. So, I want to and get to do those things as a CEO, as each conversation, each task, each action has a purpose in alignment with the bigger purpose. Now, that said, we are a team, and other people do many important things on my behalf. This creates leverage and allows me to do the things no one else has the skills or time to do.

So, you learned to say no to things not requiring you, handed them to people who are able to deliver, and freed yourself up to focus on what is aligned with your purpose in life? Is that right?

Yes and no. I want to build this business. But first, I know I need to focus on being whole—internally. I act from *Being*, but not all my actions are related to this business. As I practiced living in this optimal *being* state, I realized I was missing two big parts of my fulfillment. First, I had forgotten about my friend, Alexander, and my commitment to help others. So, now, my plan is to help 10,000 people get to where they want to go, to their purpose. First, I created a fund to realize this, and we have a volunteer team to manage it. I seeded it with $10,000, and Easy Breezy gives 5 percent of its profits to this fund. So far, we have supported twelve people, and I am thrilled with the response. We now have over $120,000 in the fund and it's growing.

Second, I had mistakenly seen people in our business as tools to get a job done. I now see the humanity in people, and we are implementing programs, policies, and culture here at Easy Breezy—like the Optimal Being program—to support their fullness of life. This has not always been easy. A few people moved on from the company since these changes, but I believe it is for the best. We now hire people passionate about their role and the environment we are fostering.

Yori, I appreciate your commitment to yourself and your purpose. I see how your actions have influenced the people I've interviewed so far. Is there anything else you want to share about this element of well-being, your use of will, and fulfilling your plans and goals?

If you are not following through on things in your life, it indicates you are saying yes to things out of alignment with your life's purposes. Stop. Check in. *Am I aligned?* is a question to ask over and over, whenever things are not going as you expect. Once you notice something is out of alignment and you can take the time to re-establish that inner connection with your optimal Being, you will have an opportunity to *tune in* to what you do want. Listen carefully to yourself in this state and take action. You will learn that you are very capable of following through.

Observe what you are doing. Stop doing things out of alignment with your best interests. How? Get into alignment and assess your current plans. Stop the ones that don't fit. Continue the ones that do. When timely, start new plans. I do all three of these things weekly, assuring my actions are aligned with my purposes. Sounds simple, right? It's not always easy. It took me a few months to reconnect with what I truly wanted.

I learned to pray and meditate pondering these questions:

1. *What do I need to be aware of regarding my purpose?*
2. *How about the company's purpose?*
3. *What plans need stopping, starting, or changing?*

4. *What goals are for today in alignment with my purposes and plans?*

Once completed, I continue my day and find, most often, my daily goals are met. Throughout the day, I check in with my internal guidance to decide which goals and plans to focus on. It's as close as I have come to my mother's conversations with God.

Brilliant! Thank you, Yori. It's been a pleasure to meet with you. I am so excited to see you continuing to support the evolution of this organization.

I look forward to reading about all these interviews. My sincere appreciation to you and your team.

He looked back over his shoulder and smiled as he walked out the door. I both saw and felt his smile. After a moment of self-reflection, I realized I was feeling *inspired*.

Interview Notes

My interview with Yori was even better than I expected. He is a heart-centered person who genuinely cares. I would definitely work for him. I think a lot of people would. What a pleasure it would be to work in the culture he is fostering!

The Well-Being Element of Use of Will

People don't leave jobs;
they leave bosses and toxic environments.

Have you heard a version of this saying? People respond to the culture they work in. The work culture consists of many parts that can focus on relationships, shared ideals, curiosity and innovation, enjoyment, results, control, safety, cooperation, and much more.[14] What if a company's leaders were committed to creating a workplace culture that supported employees as they worked to *Be* their best self while they were *Doing* the work of their jobs?

The Optimal Being program is designed to awaken the workforce to Being while they Do. When leaders implement this program and follow through on its elements, both personally and in their company roles, the benefits pour onto others, much like a cool, spring rain. Employees in this culture grow healthier and happier as they move the company forward with their best efforts, communications, and ideas.

What would this look like for your company? For your team? For your personal life?

Imagine going to work each day, knowing that you will be moving toward your purpose in life and contributing to that movement in others. It's a gamechanger!

Shifting this element in your organization has so many benefits. See more about how it plays out personally and organizationally as a challenge or when optimal by scanning this QR code with your phone's camera.

QR code URL: optimalbeing.live/well-being-info-graphic

Chapter 11

Emma: Consistency

Emma is Germanic in origin, meaning *whole* or *universal*.

Emma does not actually work at Easy Breezy. She was the first spouse of an employee to take advantage of the Optimal Being program. I looked forward to her unique perspective from outside this company.

Emma, a petite woman with short-cropped hair, wore a pants outfit with suspenders and a button-down blouse, topped off with a red-and-white polka-dot bow tie. She had a tint of blue in her hair and wore a necklace with the words *I am* resting on her chest. She cupped a coffee mug in both hands as she took a sip.

The Interview

I see you are all set. Any questions before we get started?

> Just one. Is it okay if my daughter, Helina, joins us? I want her to hear me explain what consistency really means and what it means for her future. She is in the next room. It is fine for her to watch a movie over there, but I prefer she be here if that's okay with you.

Clearly this was important to Emma, and I felt uncertain about changing the format. As is my practice, I breathed into that feeling and asked my internal GPS if Helina should join us. I immediately felt the uncertainly lift as I realized I was concerned a bit with being in control. I chuckled at myself and allowed her daughter to join.

Helina was a young teen and was clearly not enthusiastic about being there. Apparently, Emma did not fully explain why she had been dragged to the office, but here she sat. Unlike her mother, Helina had long blonde hair and wore all pink and black. She did have a matching streak of color in her hair. I noted she was trying to be different from Mom, but still connected. Emma took Helina's phone away, earning an eye roll from the teen.

Will Helina's participation influence how you answer the questions?

> Honestly, I don't know. Although, once upon a time, I could emphatically say they would. Not so much today.

Okay. Let's get started. How would you explain this element of well-being called consistency?

Well, have you ever made a cake and noticed all the ingredients have a role to play and yet are not able to play the role until you add them into the batter? And then, it's not ready to bake until they are all mixed in thoroughly. That's consistency. Once mixed, all the parts are there and important, yet each is no longer a separate part. It is no longer possible for the butter to be used on your morning toast. It is no longer possible to scramble those eggs. They are all one as the batter. The parts are all-in on being a cake. Now, imagine the cake rejecting the eggs. So, the eggs are thinking about becoming scrambled or fried or used to make French toast and believe they have the potential to be whatever they desire. Yet, they are actually in the cake!

Confusing? Yes. But think about it in terms of a person. What parts of you have you rejected? What parts have you judged? What parts have you left out, now exploring their own possibilities, searching for answers? I did that. It was my way of protecting myself, but it led to consistency being a challenge. I looked like a whole, regular person, but inside I was divided and confused.

I have a theory about why I did this. I have stories of how it affected my life, and I can explain how everything integrated back together.

I am so curious how this showed up for you, and how it affected your life. Please continue, but also include Helina, if you would. I would love to hear her perspective too.

As you wish, assuming Helina is up for that.

Helina shrugged and gave a nod. Emma nodded back and continued.

You see, I was a girl in a family of boys and was never quite sure how to fit in with other girls. Some were too prissy and some were judgmental, and others were cool, and still others were like me in some ways. When I didn't fit in well, I sought ways to fit in. I tried to make myself beautiful but didn't do it *right*. I tried to be smart and was teased for being a showoff. Then I tried to be a jock—I was called a boy. I felt like an outcast most of my youth. By the time I hit high school, I was totally confused about who I was.

Since kids my age didn't like me, I was determined not to screw things up at home. I started behaving the way I thought my parents wanted me to and continued doing that, afraid if I didn't, they might reject me as my peers had. I went for *perfect daughter* as a goal, and that seemed to work. Meanwhile, I still tried to be liked at school. After all, in my mind, my family didn't have choice about liking me, and I wanted real people to like me too.

That played out through college and into my career. Though the core of me was me, I would adjust my conversation, my beliefs, and my behavior depending on who I was with. This led me to betray and reject myself again and again. My mid-life crisis was a crisis of who I was. Was I the party girl who danced on tables? I was when I was with Natasha and Drew. Was I the girl who gossiped about her boss? I was with certain people, and every time, I felt I needed a purifying shower after. Was I the career woman who put work ahead of family? I was if my husband was not around and my boss was asking for extra hours. I put myself in so many uncomfortable situations by changing into who I needed to be to satisfy my desire for acceptance.

I had many relationship *bank accounts* and was over-drawn on the most important relationships in my life: family.

Helina had a tear forming, and I realized she was one of the overdrawn accounts. As her single tear fell, Emma put a hand gently on her leg and continued.

I was inconsistent, unreliable—hated by some and adored by others. I would make and then undo decisions, and then I'd second-guess myself again, unaware of what I actually wanted and afraid to find out. The charade I was living fell apart when I lost my job. I faced my husband and kids and realized I owed them more than was possible to repay.

That was when I was introduced to the Optimal Being program. As you know, I don't work here, but my husband does. He told me about this awakened workforce concept that was kicking off. He laughed about it and said it was stupid but left the link open on our home computer. It was exactly what I needed. I called him at work and asked if family members could participate. They could for a fee, but that didn't matter. I was in.

You were the first spouse in the program here, weren't you?

Yes, and I was so scared to be with all Mike's work people, but it ended up being perfect. In fact, after a while Mike signed up and no longer believes it's stupid. He has his wife back, after all.

Back?

Yes. He has me at my best. I am clear on who I am. I no longer try to please people like I did. I am clear on my beliefs and what I want. It was remarkable to discover that I hadn't considered my own desires because they might have conflicted with the desires of others, and I couldn't risk being rejected in any way. I was such a horrible employee before getting clear. I was essentially useless.

How so?

I am exaggerating a bit, but compared to now, I was ineffective. I either made quick choices that fit what people wanted, or I would take forever to make a decision if it was on me alone. I'd research and get opinions and research some more and finally make decisions that were not ideal. You see, I would choose based on which way the wind was blowing, if you know that saying. It didn't matter if my choice went against my own instincts. I cost my company so much time, money, and energy, and then would make a decision that was not even what I thought was best.

It caught up to me. I was out of work all the while doing this program. I wouldn't have it any other way, though. I now know I chose my career to please what I thought Mom wanted for me. Now, I am exploring what I love and have found what I want. I'm going for it!

She looked at Helina, inviting her to speak.

Yeah, my mom is becoming a dog groomer and opening her own business. A far cry from accounting.

Helina finished with another eye roll and added a head shake. Emma continued.

My mom wanted to make sure I could financially support myself in case I ever got married and it didn't work out. She preached independence to me my whole life while a number of her friends found themselves divorced and lacking any marketable skills. Accounting was practical and paid well. Unfortunately, numbers and I were not friends, and it was hard for me to keep up with my coworkers. Fun, it was not.

Helina chimed in.

Yeah, if you haven't heard her quote Yoda yet, you will.

Helina, what is your take on your mom's changes?

Well, she's nicer. And she seems happier. She says what she wants more. And, I would say now her *yes* means *yes* and her *no* means *no*. I never used to know whether she was being honest with me. I guess that's because she was not honest with herself, right? I prefer honesty. My life is the opposite. I know what I want.

I just wish she could have figured it out sooner. It's hard to watch my younger siblings get her now when I had to deal with the old her for most of my life. She was so fake. She was always going to help some friend who needed help, telling us it was for *our* benefit. I think helping other people made her feel important or something.

But, we kids knew we were last in her life. I hope this lasts 'cause I don't want to go back to that.

Tears fell for both women as the conversation paused. I watched Emma take deep breaths, internally practicing the techniques she learned in the program. I joined her breathing, giving her the time needed to process the moment. Finally, I spoke.

What do you think, Emma?

She answered to Helina.

Oh, honey. I know you feel resentment. Thank you for saying that. I can't do anything except show up consistently to prove that it will last. I will keep practicing these tools and mixing the batter, so to speak. I can tell you the number-one benefit: I have discovered I have a beautiful and amazing family that I will cherish all the days of my life.

I am proud of how clear you are about who you are, and I brought you here to learn from me. Now, I realize I am learning from you. Thank you.

A smile crossed Helina's face for the first time since the interview started.

Emma, now that you are more consistent in your own life, what is it you want?

In addition to pet grooming, I want to help more and more people be clear about who they are. I want them to live as their highest selves. I believe they can live at the highest level of their ability—the biggest gap is inside them.

I'm excited about living these principles and being an example to my daughter—to all our kids. I have gone from being insecure and second-guessing everything to being clear and consistent. I think for myself now for the first time since preschool. The confidence is exhilarating!

People who struggle with this element often second-guess their decisions as you mentioned. Can you tell us more?

Yes, I felt pulled in multiple directions and couldn't choose. I looked busy to people, but that didn't mean I was productive. Now, I can see the difference. Before, I would have argued I was *doing my best* and would have actually believed it because I didn't have anything to compare it to. My issue was hidden, but now I *know*.

People with this challenge are untrustworthy. I was untrustworthy. Until it is addressed and corrected, it is impossible to count on these people over an extended period of time. Why? They change as soon as the wind changes because they are inconsistent on the inside.

If a person is willing to explore this element of consistency, it can go from a challenge to a strength. I can attest to that.

I wouldn't say it's easy to accept, but it is addressable.

Thank you for this interview. I know the rest of the interviewees were employees and I just really appreciate being included.

Emma winked at Helina, who was now sitting up and fully engaged in the conversation.

Any last thoughts, Helina?

I like how you are now, Mom. Please stay this way!

Emma's tears streamed, and Helina hugged her mom.

Interview Notes

The joy on Emma's face will be etched in my mind for some time to come. Priceless. Priceless. What an enjoyable and rewarding experience these interviews have been. I admit to being uncertain about Helina joining our interview, but thankfully, I listened to my internal guidance and we all reaped the benefits.

The Well-Being Element of Consistency

The element often shows up as a challenge in the following behaviors:

- Questioning self
- Unable to form opinions without validation
- Going along with others without self-assessing
- Procrastination
- Indecision
- Placing approval above other considerations
- Always willing to compromise
- Unable to state personal values or desire

There is a study by a group called Correlated that states 53 percent of employees tend to second-guess their decisions.[15] I'm guessing every one of them has this challenge of consistency. Another study (by Forel) points to this challenge showing up as procrastination. Apparently, 80 percent of salaried workers procrastinate one to four hours per day.[16]

If this is true in your workplace, what does this tell you about productivity and cost-effectiveness?

Shifting this element in your organization has so many benefits. See more about how it plays out personally and organizationally as a challenge or when optimal by scanning this QR code with your phone's camera.

QR code URL: optimalbeing.live/well-being-info-graphic

Final Notes

You have heard from Harmony (Stress), Caron (Others), Roma (Self), Alethia (Truth), Jabari (Fear), Ping (Hostility), Tarina (Universal Law), Ozzie (Physical Vitality), Yori (Use of Will/Goals), Emma (Consistency), and Helina (the Next Generation). As you moved through these pages, did you see yourself in some of our participants? Imagine how your coworkers might also see themselves in these examples of lives changed for their optimal good.

In my years of serving as a Guide and Mentor in this program, I have witnessed a multitude of transformations in individuals and their workplaces. I am still filled with gratitude and awe by each journey I have the privilege to witness. The journey to live as the best of ourselves leads to the best in all of us. The journey is worth taking.

Inspired to explore this program for your company and/ or for yourself? We are here for you, ready to support your awakened workforce. I look forward to meeting you.

Ethan

P.S. Ethan is the name I chose for this project. It means *wisdom* and *strength*.

The Program

Awakening Your Optimal Workforce

Is employee well-being a priority for you and your organization?

Awakening Your Optimal Workforce implements the tools and principles of the Optimal Being program. This tried-and-true series of educational materials, application tools, and mentorship is available for teams, individuals, groups, and companies to experience. To begin, representatives from your company meet with Optimal Being team leaders and explore your organization's objectives. Then, these ten elements of well-being that you have experienced through these interviews are assessed in your workplace. The results reveal clearly where strengths and issues exist.

Once your company's objectives are defined, the program is implemented with individual employees. Each participant takes an assessment to determine areas of strength and challenge. Then, the Optimal Being program—the core curriculum for your Awakened Workforce—provides material to explore through multiple media, focusing on each participant's top three of ten challenge elements. A Program Guide interacts with participants to support optimal results, and weekly group mentoring sessions are available to dive deeper and practice. At the end of the program, participants take the assessment again, which reveals a fresh set of top challenges to which the tools may be applied next.

Companies who implement this program will have a workforce more in alignment than out of alignment. Though each organization will experience unique benefits to them, benefits others celebrate include: A workplace that is attractive and inviting. Productivity increases, and issues, such as absenteeism and low morale, decrease. Employees experience better health and balance in their work environment and in their personal lives. The benefits of this program continue to expand with time as relationships heal, leaders grow, and communications improve.

Beyond the program delivering highly statistically significant modifications in behavior, it's easy and rather enjoyable.

Consider an approach that can make a difference in the fabric of your organization supporting well-being for all.

To learn more please visit optimalbeing.live or contact us at wellbeing@optimalbeing.live to discuss your specifics.

We look forward to meeting with you.

Acknowledgments

I would like to show sincere appreciation for three groups of people for their assistance with the book in your hands: Loved Ones, Book People, and Work People.

Let's begin with Loved Ones:

My wife, Liz, is doing something in our home today, Saturday, and letting me write, allowing me the freedom to create and do what I thoroughly enjoy doing. There are many Saturdays, late nights, and days when she would much rather have me helping out at home, yet she shows up in supportive ways. Today is one of those days, and I appreciate all of it in this moment.

Children are marvelous reflections of love, showing us what we most need to see and showing us the areas we might attempt to keep hidden. Our five children showed up in this world as pure love. I attempt to see them always in that way. Below are five quick stories, one for each of them. These are by no means exhaustive reflections of these amazing human beings, just moments in time I believe you can appreciate with me.

Charlie showed me that miracles actually can happen. His ear healing from a major catastrophe at four years old was an opportunity for me to witness something I had only read or heard stories about previously. He demonstrated faith and the healing that came was a moment of awe for Liz and me.

John showed up with the patience of a master when I was out of my mind and gently reminded me through the years when I was "off." He did it with such grace and love.

David showed me the freedom of spirit in his playfulness with life, reminding me to let go and allow life to be.

Henry had two powerful and contrasting expressions in his support of our family growing. First, I was hiding anger and hurt and sadness and hid it as well as I could. Henry would reveal how to show it. He was a perfect expression of everything I had stuffed. He helped me see it was okay to show my emotions and accept them. He also was a gift in supporting my ability to tell stories effectively. His invitation to tell him stories created a gift for growth that I am still in awe of and appreciate so much.

Sophie used to come into my office and teach me. She called it "God school." I would ask her questions, and when she was just three, she would teach me who I was in relationship with the idea I had of God. She helped me realize it was not a *man in the clouds* as I held to in my youth, but it was a force of love in all of creation, including in each of us. Appropriately named Sophie, known to mean Wisdom, I will forever remember my classroom experience with her.

I grew up in a family who modeled love and support, with my parents and four sisters and the many aunts, uncles, cousins, and of course, grandparents. If the world ever presented its cruel teeth, my family was always a rock where I could anchor myself to and find refuge. With so many who do not have this experience, I acknowledge my ancestry and the commitment to being present as love, especially when someone faulters, fails, or struggles. We have proven again and again that we will always be there with and for each other. Thank you!

Let's continue with Book People:

Books take time and effort by many people. It begins with words on a page and over time is developed and modified to become a finished work. This particular book is possible due to the following active participants:

Keith Leon offered up a gift to me in the form of Karen Burton being part of this project. Karen and I spent many hours online and through email and shared documents refining the original draft. During that process, Rex Montague-Bauer and Paul Repicky read and modified the draft Karen worked from, and then reviewed anything asked throughout the process. I also want to thank Colleen McHugh who helped inspire this by sharing her HR expertise as Rex, Paul, and I were navigating how to most effectively present the ten elements of well-being for a corporate audience.

Additionally, Tom McCauley, John Golden, and Michael Englehardt offered relevant insights at just the right time during the writing process. Special thanks go out as well to Mandy and Alex Doman, who fully embraced bringing the Optimal Being program into their organization at an early stage of its corporate development. They—along with the many graduates over the years, including dozens of participants from the Powerful-U community—were essential to inspiring the stories found in these pages. Thank you to James and Steph Purpura for sharing this with your community.

Others who played a less direct role in the writing process, but without whom this book would not be possible:

Michael J. Ryce (whyagain.org). Michael taught me about a set of tools based in a concept called the *Personal Code* that he and Dr. Dan McDougal put into a powerful assessment over fifty years ago. This is the backdrop for the tools that inspired how to help people realize what the ten elements of well-being are and how to *move the needle* in life from out of alignment with an element to in alignment. Thank you to Michael and all who have contributed over the years to this set of principles and tools so essential for living an optimal life.

Let's wrap up with Work People:

I have come across countless people in my life, yet a few stand out as having influenced my reason for writing this book. My cousin, Joel Basgall, was my first business partner. Joel and I built Geneca, a company that was first and foremost a people company. We chose to treat everyone—employees, contractors, vendors, customers—as best as possible. Of course, we failed again and again, yet we kept at it and made choices that generally were aligned with the best interests of people. This led to Geneca receiving awards again and again for being one of the very best places to work in Chicago, as well as statewide.

Despite our success at that time, it was only later that I learned about the principles I write about in this book. I know we could do even better today. It is this inspiration that led to my persistence in writing this book through the highs and lows.

I want people like Joel and me, who genuinely care about people and their well-being, to have resources that are meaningful, effective, and relatively simple to implement. I want other leaders to know resources exist to support your moving beyond "check the box" solutions that often fall short of truly impacting someone's life. Thank you to all you leaders who care.

I have the pleasure of working with a few of those leaders now. Much appreciation goes to our team at *Journey's Dream*, including Breaha Wallin, Mitzi Montague-Bauer, Rex Montague-Bauer, Dr. Timothy Hayes, Aimee Canfield, Brenda Steinberger-Domienik, Dr. Albert Mensah, Dr. Paul Repicky, Chase Austin, Joseph Gabriel, Celina Ruhala, Denise Coelho, Angie Bruce, Nick Hankes, and so many more advisors, partners, supporters, and advocates! It is such a pleasure to work with all of you.

A Letter to Leaders

Dear Leader,

Everyone is responsible for their own life. Everyone has in them innate intelligence to make moment to moment choices aligned with what is optimal for them in any given moment.

That said, some strategies are more effective than others. A person who wishes to heal from a painful memory and experience may drown their painful issues with strategies that are destructive in other ways. The difference between dying and surviving may be what is right in front of them, a drug, alcohol, anger, running and hiding, fighting and winning, and so on. These are concepts that are all too familiar and fail in the long term as we have seen. Drink your troubles away too many times and you have found that it is not easy to stop. Devoid of an alternative, who would want to? Now, let's explore where you come in.

At your company, some employees thrive. Others tread water, struggling to keep afloat. Still others may have mastered the art of floating, yet no one can float forever. Eventually, they may sink. The ones in your company who are sinking are doing their best to find resources, and you can be an advocate. Coming from someone who has experienced sinking, floating, and thriving, I can tell you the resources companies rely on now are inadequate for today's workforce.

The healthcare stuff is too late. By then, your people are in it and need critical care to get back to floating. The other resources are often Band-Aids at best and provide temporary relief.

What people want is a real solution. Moving beyond issues affecting well-being requires inner tools that support us when our shit is up.

Good solutions do exist, and the pages of this book highlight an approach that works. Benefit you and your workforce. Give them a copy of this book. Read it yourself. Share it with others. Let people know that living optimally is possible now.

Keep your other strategies. Keep the Monday morning yoga lessons, keep the protocols for health plans, and keep what you have that works. Add to this so people are making the better choices for them in a given moment. This will lead them to make the best choices for you and your organization.

You may be thinking that you didn't sign up to lead people by caring for their well-being. However, this is the responsibility of twenty-first-century leaders. Give your people the tools they most need, and you will get everything you ever wanted. And more.

In sincerest appreciation for all you are doing.

Mark Hattas
CEO and Co-Creator of the Optimal Being program

About the Author

Mark Hattas is the CEO and cofounder of Rookha Group, Inc., creator of the Optimal Being program. He also co-founded Journey's Dream, a powerful health and well-being 501c3 charity. Mark is an Optimal Being Executive Mentor, certified Extreme Focus mental performance coach, and certified teacher in Personal Code Assessment and Dr. Michael Ryce programs, including "Why Is This Happening to Me . . . Again?!"

Mark started, built, and sold Geneca, a technology services company reaching a workforce of nearly 150 people and $20 million in revenue, before launching ventures supporting optimal living. These ventures were inspired by Mark overcoming a major mental illness and his commitment to support others in thriving. His low point in 2014 remains etched as a memory in support of compassion for others who face challenges today. His healing process began as a result of using the tools discussed in this book.

Mark and his teams bring solutions that make a difference in the lives of anyone who touches and uses the solutions. For nearly a decade, he and his teammates have invested millions of dollars in time, money, and resources to create solutions for others to benefit and transform their lives at the optimum level. We have all seen the devastation of lives when people don't have tools in support of their optimal well-being. Mark and his teammates are committed to making these resources available to everyone.

Mark is co-author of the number-one international bestseller *Journeys to Success: Wellness and Fitness Edition*, and author of *Awakening the Optimal Leader*, the children's book, *IT*, *Awakening Your Optimal Workforce*, and *Prisoner of War* (as John Aconda).

Mark carries the highest endorsement by the number-one ranked Business Conference in the World (by 3rd party press, 2010–2020), whose founder, Berny Dohrmann (mentor to thought leaders like Tony Robbins, Jack Canfield, and superstar Bob Proctor of *The Secret*), calls Mark "Teacher of the Masters, who is bringing in new truth and frequency right when human awareness can embrace its urgent upgrading," and claims a session with Mark is worth $100,000 at market rates.

Mark believes every human has a right to live their optimal life. He is here to support all in doing this.

Mark lives in the Chicago area, sharing this adventure of life with his wonderful wife, Liz, their five children, and two pet cats.

You can also contact him through:

Awakened Workforce and Optimal Living – optimalbeing. live

Sustained Mental Health – journeysdream.org

Endnotes

1. National Council for Mental Wellbeing, "What Is the State of America's Mental Health?" thenationalcouncil.org/policy-action/what-is-the-state-of-americas-mental-health/#foobox-1/4/071519_NCBH_AMHSocial_InfoE.png.

2. Cosette Taillac, "Mental Health at Work: Creating a Stigma-Free Culture," (March 18, 2019), business.kaiserpermanente.org/insights/mental-health-workplace/supporting-mental-health.

3. David Sturt and Todd Nordstrom, "10 Shocking Workplace Stats You Need To Know," *Forbes*, (March 8, 2018), www.forbes.com/sites/davidsturt/2018/03/08/10-shocking-workplace-stats-you-need-to-know/#7bf1be9af3af.

4. American Psychiatric Association, "About Half of Workers Are Concerned About Discussing Mental Health Issues in the Workplace; A Third Worry About Consequences If They Seek Help," (May 20, 2019) psychiatry.org/newsroom/news-releases/about-half-of-workers-are-concerned-about-discussing-mental-health-issues-in-the-workplace-a-third-worry-about-consequences-if-they-seek-help.

5. Charlotte Lieberman, "What Wellness Programs Don't Do for Workers," *Harvard Business Review*, (August 14,

2019), hbr.org/2019/08/what-wellness-programs-dont-do-for-workers.

6. Center for Creative Leadership. "Why (and How) to Confront Problem Employees." ccl.org/articles/leading-effectively-articles/confront-problem-employees/

7. Beheshti, Naz. "10 Timely Statistics About The Connection Between Employee Engagement And Wellness." *Forbes*. 16 January 2019. forbes.com/sites/nazbeheshti/2019/01/16/10-timely-statistics-about-the-connection-between-employee-engagement-and-wellness/?sh=55ba251c22a0

8. Society for Human Research Management. "Navigating COVID-19: Impact of the Pandemic on Mental Health," (*National survey conducted* April 15–16, 2020), shrm.org/hr-today/trends-and-forecasting/research-and-surveys/Documents/SHRM%20CV19%20Mental%20Health%20Research%20Presentation%20v1.pdf.

9. DOE Nuclear Air Cleaning Handbook. 11 Dec 2003, page 6-2. encrypted-tbn0.gstatic.com/images?q=tbn:ANd9GcRhLruXwhFD4CARXtRp-X9bSmPnPv-dpe5H3g&usqp=CAU

10. Young, Stephen, Glazer, Jessica, and Sydney Siver. "Problem Employees: Identify and Manage Them Before They Impact Your Business and Career. *Center for Creative Leadership*. April 2018. cclinnovation.org/wp-content/uploads/2020/02/problem-employees-ccl-white-paper.pdf?web-

SyncID=d4b5098b-5ae7-d22a-ddb3-b341d7e9e832&sessionGUID=b5902dd9-33aa-ad7c-778e-2c57918a53c7

11. Marcia McReynolds, "Statistics on Listening," Listening Planet, thelisteningcards.com/statistics.

12. Christopher Bader, et al., "Fear Itself: The Causes and Consequences of Fear in America," Chapman University chapman.edu/wilkinson/research-centers/babbie-center/survey-american-fears.aspx.

13. King, Martin Luther, Jr. "Advice for Living." *The Martin Luther King, Jr. Research and Education Institute*, Stanford University. October 1957. kinginstitute.stanford.edu/king-papers/documents/advice-living-2

14. Boris Groysberg et al., "The Leader's Guide to Corporate Culture: How to Manage the Eight Critical Elements of Organizational Life," *Harvard Business Review*, (January–February 2018), hbr.org/2018/01/the-leaders-guide-to-corporate-culture.

15. Correlated, "People Who Tend to Second-Guess Their Decisions," correlated.org/1529.

16. Darius Foroux, "How Common Is Procrastination?" dariusforoux.com/wp-content/uploads/2019/06/How-Common-Is-Procrastination-A-Study-By-Darius-Foroux.pdf.